THE PLAYS OF EUGENE O'NEILL

A CRITICAL STUDY

THE PLAYS OF EUGENE O'NEILL

A CRITICAL STUDY

Monika Gupta

ATLANTIC
PUBLISHERS & DISTRIBUTORS (P) LTD

Published by

ATLANTIC

PUBLISHERS & DISTRIBUTORS (P) LTD

7/22, Ansari Road, Darya Ganj,
New Delhi-110002
Phones : +91-11-40775252, 23273880, 23275880, 23280451
Fax : +91-11-23285873
Web : www.atlanticbooks.com
E-mail : orders@atlanticbooks.com

Branch Office
5, Nallathambi Street, Wallajah Road,
Chennai-600002
Phones : +91-44-64611085, 32413319
E-mail : chennai@atlanticbooks.com

Printed in India at Nice Printing Press, A-33/3A, Site-IV,
Industrial Area, Sahibabad, Ghaziabad, U.P.

PREFACE

Eugene O'Neill (1888-1953) is one of the most outstanding playwrights of the twentieth century. He has a special position in America, and is as much a playwright of international stature in the world theatre of the first half of the twentieth century as Chekhov, Shaw, Pirandello and Brecht. He shaped the course of American Drama in the most significant period of its development, *i.e.,* from 1915 to 1930.

A survey of the critical material on O'Neill makes it evident that editors, critics and scholars have most often been led by partisanship in their approach to his plays. They are either very laudatory or violently antagonistic; few are "balanced." The plays of O'Neill touch something fundamental in those who expose themselves to their effect. They reach down to frightening depths; they step on private, social, religious, philosophical and aesthetic issues; they either evoke immoderate enthusiasm or provoke immoderate anger. Almost everyone of his plays has produced warring factions, whose representatives have often been led to express themselves in categorical terms. In the January 1960 issue of *Theatre Arts* Louis Kronenberger observed that *Long Day's Journey into Night* was "The great event in the American theatre of the 50's." But, writing in the same year, William L. Sharp lamented that "The popularity of Eugene O'Neill, who cannot write at all," arrested "the insensitive ear not only of the playwright and his audience but also the dramatic critic as well" *(Tulane Drama Review*, winter, 1960). And Gunther Crack, reviewing a performance of *Strange Interlude* in Berlin, exclaimed that "The play could only have been written by O'Neill who combines great theatrical talent with an enormous knowledge of the human soul" (*Cultural News from Germany,* April 1961). This battle of the critics regarding the importance of O'Neill is not over; he remains essentially a controversial playwright.

O'Neill is a great tragic artist, whose vision of life and human soul is fundamentally tragic. His plays are known for their tragic beauty and sublimity. There are modern tragedies which strike at the very root of the sickness of the present day world. O'Neill is not an "ivory-towerist" or an escapist in the romantic sense of the term. Being an existentialist, he deals with life in a very realistic and authentic manner. He visualises life as full of hope and promise and concludes that there is nothing wrong or repulsive about it. He pleads for the total acceptance of life at its face value. His interest in life is not limited to the realization of eternity, but is centred upon making it more meaningful and worth-living. As a dramatist, his commitment is to the faithful dramatization of human situation.

O'Neill himself has remarked : 'The playwright must dig at the roots of the sickness today as he feels it.' The feeling of isolation, which has become the hallmark of the modern age, springs from the tragic sense of life. It is variously described as loss of identity, loneliness, alienation, meaninglessness, loss of faith or values, rootlessness, anomie or anxiety-state, etc. It is recognized as a symptom of man's contemporary crisis, a human problem, a condition of having the experience but missing the meaning. In the contemporary experience, it refers to a dis-relationship between the self and its world, the reduction of man to the status of a thing, the insoluble conflict of the self between the pleasure and reality principle, the loss of the feeling of being an active determining force in his own life, and the unbridgeable gulf between reason and experience, the self and the non-self.

Man suffers and his life becomes a tale of isolation, loneliness and estrangement, ending with the cessation of his earthly life neither because of the hostility of Fate as in the Greek tragedy, nor of *Hamartia* in his character. Instead, he suffers from the sense of alienation because of his loss of faith in some supernatural power of traditional religions, a faith which the Greeks had, and which Christianity supplied in the Middle Ages, but which has been eroded by science or materialism today. The old religions have not been replaced by the new ones. Hence, man's soul is sick because of too much materialism, and he suffers from inner emptiness on account of his lack of some sustaining faith. He feels orphaned, lonely and at bay. His agony arises from a feeling or 'insecurity' a feeling of 'not-belonging,' and he is confused and bewildered from within and from without.

Materialistic values prevail, and hence life has become too mechanical and impersonal, it has further shaken man's sense of security. This feeling of insecurity and isolation causes inbearable spiritual anguish, fear and torture. Sometimes, as in the case of Brutus Jones in *Emperor Jones* and Yank in *The Hairy Ape,* it becomes a terrible obsession which brings them to their doom. In play after play, O'Neill's characters are stretched on the rack, suffering the tortures of Hell. The rack on which he stretches his characters could be the past life, and the tornment could come from man's sense of being separated from Nature, of not 'belonging' to the universe as in *The Hairy Ape.* Again, the soul may be tortured by 'not belonging' to the old supernatural God, or to the new scientific God represented by the machine as in *Dynamo*. It may also come from 'not belonging' to oneself and to any all-fulfilling love as in *Strange Interlude*, or from 'not belonging' incestuously to a forbidden object as in *Mourning Becomes Electra*.

Again, this feeling of isolation may arise from the 'romantic illusion' which some may harbour. Lost in the 'romantic illusion,' they forget the reality of life, which, ultimately lead them to their doom. In *Iceman Cometh*, each of the characters has his own 'pipe-dream' which is the cause of his undoing. The tragic tension and isolation may be caused by the Puritan ideals, which are basically a negation of life, an inhibition of natural instincts and impulses as in *Mourning Becomes Electra*. Whatever form such escape from life may take, it is always a cause of isolation and suffering.

Social environment is also an important factor for man's isolated state and agony. In *The Hairy Ape*, Yank is a man as well as worker, brutalized and mechanized by an impersonal and mechanical social order. Racial discrimination and slum-life in *Christie*, granding and improverished farm-life in *Beyond the Horizon,* partriarchal authority at its extreme and the struggle for land in *Desire Under the Elms,* extreme family pride, joy-denying puritanism and mercantile possessiveness are all the causes of isolation, suffering and tragedy.

Basically and essentially, O'Neill's plays are the embodiments of a cosmic anguish. As he himself says, he has studied man not in relation to man, but man in relation to God. Living in an impersonal, mechanical, urbanized and industrialized social environment, man today is alienated from God, traditions and religions of the past, Nature and his fellow beings. He suffers from loss of identity, inner emptiness, isolation, normlessness, powerlessness and sense of insecurity. Thus, isolation and loneliness, man's disorientation, or man's bewilderment from within and from without are the major themes in the plays of O'Neill. The present book, which is a revised version of my Ph.D. Thesis, is an attempt to examine his plays critically.

Words cannot express my gratitude to Prof. S.S. Deo, Head, Department of English, Modern European and Other Foreign Languages, H.N.B. Garhwal University, Srinagar, Garhwal, to whom I owe this book. It was his encouragement which enabled me to bring the work in the present shape. I am highly grateful to my teacher, Dr. M.L. Trivedi, Retd. Head, Department of English, P.P.N. College, Kanpur, whose role has certainly been the most decisive in incepting and completing this work. I am thankful to Dr. B.D. Pandey, Reader, Department of English, P.P.N. College, Kanpur, for his valuable suggestions from time to time. For providing me with the study-material, I am thankful to Prof. H.C. Choudhary, Head, Department of English, Christ Church College, Kanpur, the Librarian, ASRC, Hyderabad, and the Central Library, I.I.T., Kanpur. I owe a deep sense of gratitude to my father, Sri R.S. Gupta, formerly Registrar, H.N.B. Garhwal University, Srinagar, Garhwal, and my mother, Mrs. Nandini Gupta, for their constant encouragement, help and blessings. Lastly, I must thank my husband, Satish and my dear daughter, Poorva without whose co-operation it would have never been possible for me to stay on this research plan. Finally, I am thankful to all those who have assisted me in the completion of this book.

MONIKA GUPTA

CONTENTS

1

Introduction

The creative career of Eugene O'Neill (1888-1953) spanned the crucial period between the two World Wars. The period of three decades from 1914 to 1945 was charged with intense dramatic potential which O'Neill used to good advantage by writing some highly stimulating plays. His works reveal a varied and colorful and thematic and structural spectrum. They touch upon a large variety of themes, and show theatrical experimentation with virtually all sorts of devices and patterns. Even in size and shape, his plays range from very short plays to those of epic dimension. His works, thus, show a restless and creative spirit at work. This is so because he never felt at home in the socio-cultural and economic milieu of the capitalist-materialist culture of grab-and-loot around him. He always aspired to a life of creative fulfilment, which he was denied in a country that in the name of individual freedom and equality only perpetuated a philosophy of bondage, elitism and an all-pervasive jungle-law carrying the fancy name of *laissez-faire*.

O'Neill is a critic of the American society of this kind, and also of society as a whole. He thinks of man in relation to his social system. It is not man as an individual alone that concerns him but man in his social order — tortured, starved, disillusioned, disappointed and driven to disaster by the forces of system which cares nothing for the jungle welfare of this society. He treats man not as a free, detached individual, not merely as an individual in relation to a few characters, but as a person against the background of social forces. It is the social implication that makes O'Neill's plays lively in the minds of the audience. His importance as a social critic lies in the fact that he emphasizes the psychological aspects of modern and social set-up. He points out the disease of America's acquisitive society. He does not merely stress the fact that workers are exploited to create wealth for the few, but shows how in our modern, machine-made world they are deprived of the sense of harmony and mental well-being. Man's work is a necessary part of his personality; it is an expression of his ego and makes him feel that he is a necessary part of the life of the world in which he lives. Modern industry tends to destory this psychological counterpart of work, and leaves the worker a nervous, irritable and dissatisfying misfit in the society.

A man of firm conviction, O'Neill never feels shy of discussing American society in a free and frank manner. He does not see eye to eye with those, who indulge in the false glorification of the American society and blindly hail it as flawless. No wonder he said in 1946 : "I am going on the theory that the United States, instead of being the most successful country in the world, is the greatest failure."[1] His social perspective covers an aspect of modern American society, in particular, and his plays embody the ideas and conflicts of the first half of the twentieth century and deal with the social and economic issues of our time — materialism, industrialization, human-relation, employer-employee conflicts, ignorance, brutality, selfishness, greed, hatred, etc. One of the most leading problems of the human society today is the situation of man in it. O'Neill is at his best in the superb handling of this problem : the theme of 'belongingness' in the present world. For him, man remains a searcher with no clear-cut destination. He has no place in the highly industrialized set-up of modern society, and remains as an outsider, an alienated person from the beginning to the end of his life. He has lost the centre, and moves from pillar to post in search of some centre of 'belonging,' but he fails to find root anywhere. And it is quite ironical that man, who in responsible for changing the very complexion of society on earth, has no place in it. He has fallen prey to a cosmic anguish. Seen in relation to God, he has lost faith in the Gods of old religions, and has found no new faith. Living in an impersonal, mechanical, urbanized and industrialized social environment, he is constantly on the rack. He suffers from inner emptiness, isolation and feeling of insecurity and, thus, is bedeviled from within and without. In other words, isolation from the society, loneliness and search for identity constitute the basic theme of O'Neill's plays.

Man has lost the sense of harmony in nature, and is unable to establish harmony with his fellowmen. Naturally, his work has grown soulless and mechanical and he feels lonely and isolated, a mere insignificant part of a big machine, and not a human being busy in creative and purposeful activity. This mechanical life of man has led him to the loss of human identity. Isolated from their immediate environment and feeling lonely and unhappy, O'Neill's characters constantly search for identity and belongingness, and when they fail to achieve their identity, they disintegrate and decay.

There has never been a generation in the course of human history with so little ground under its feet as the modern generation. Antagonism to society has become a way of life, and there looms the reality of crisis — complex and cumulative. Nothing can avoid this crisis — neither dialectical materialism and triumphant technology, nor the undivinely and dissatisfied youth of today. In fact, multiple fears have become the foundation of the twentieth-century society. This feeling is shared alike by all. Out of step with nature, with self, and with the laws of evolutionary growth, the modern man has gone out of focus. At the very hour of its grandest victory, when it had achieved the supreme conquest over material things, the world civilization turned into a tragedy, *i.e.,* into the spiritual crisis of modern man. The modern man, who for long pitied his ancient and medieval fathers, is now himself to be pitied; he is a misfit in a world he himself has created. Torn between what man is and what he ought to be, he, living in an 'Age of Anxiety,' is forced to become aware of himself. Along with the disappearance of accepted traditional norms, moral values seem to have gone overboard. Human-engineering and future shocks have created unheard-of situations. Opportunism and irresponsibility never grew so wild as today. The fear of solitude is one of the hidden fears of man. We live among lonely crowds. The notion of estrangement and isolation is a natural corollary to the idea of relationship with others. Isolation has many facets, such as isolation from self, from others, from God and from Nature. The individual feels isolated from all human institutions like state, government etc., which have become innermost centres of power beyond the understanding or grasp of man. This is the cause of frustration and anxiety in modern man. But, in spite of his isolation and loneliness, he is in constant search of his true self.

Owing to the pressure of society, man is forced to live in a self-estranged state. In the modern technological and material society, everything becomes a problem to be solved by reasoning and calculation. "Having" becomes more important than "being" — man is possessed with car, house, pleasure, pain, etc., and this is the source of his isolation because by the hold on the things we have, we are actually under their hold. There are two extremes of 'isolation' between which a self springs : the one is a complete break from God and society, and the other is that where all sense of 'self' is lost. There is also the isolation from other because we can never totally understand them. Thus, isolation and loneliness can never be removed from our heritage and is the great ill of modern age.

The concept of isolation is the result of man's absolute freedom in facing a situation. Isolation, whether religious or secular, is always a psychological state of mind when one is cut-off from all ties, and is compelled to exercise his freedom in the face of the absurd and meaningless world. Marlowe's Doctor Faustus experienced isolation from religion and cried out for a drop of Christ's blood. Karl Marx's labour experiences secular isolation on the eve of deciding to throw himself body and soul into the class-struggle. Behind all this lies the paralysing state of mind when one is, as Sartre put it, "condemmed to be free."

The existentialist philosophical thoughts share certain concepts of "isolation" aside from their insistence on "existence" or "essence" as the central question. They regard the material or outside world as "absurd" and take a contemptuous view of history, economics and politics, asserting that nothing real or basic can be learnt from them. All posit their concept of freedom and the separation of individual from society. The individual, however, does not withdraw to monastery or cave, but carries his personal despair, or existential predicament wherever he goes, and must exhort others to see life similary. He is not free from society, but is engaged in it as a self-proclaimed "outsider" Soren Kierkegaared's remark, "The whole of existence frightens me ... the most inexplicable thing of all my own existence,"[2] is applicable to the man of the present generation. The world is to him something implacably hostile, instead of being a place where he can stretch his wings and grow. Man is to be "saved" by recognizing that the world is "absurd" and must be countered by a faith itself "absurd."

Again, Kierkegaard attacks "worldliness" :

> What is called worldliness is made up of just such men who (if one may use this expression) pawn themselves to the world. They use their talents, accumulate money, carry on worldly affairs, calculate shrewdly, etc., etc., are perhaps mentioned in history, but themselves they are not; spiritually understood, they have no self, no

> self for whose sake they could venture everything....[3]

Kierkegaard discards all worldly affairs not only greedy profit seekers but also those whose talents run to other ways — to science, to art, to the expansion of boundaries of knowledge, to the liberation of people from oppression, misery and poverty. Worldliness means attention to this world. And the penalty for worldliness is despair, isolation, estrangement, loneliness and the sickness onto death. The modern American man has no limits to his ambition; he is pragmatic, restless, energetic, ambitious, self-centred, and lives in a world of illusion. Substitution of human values by material comforts, constant need of adjustment to the changed situation, the acceptance of the image of material success as the only worthwhile goal of life make the average man a prey to a sense of inferiority, anxiety, insecurity. Hence his lonely world is populated by illusion.

Eugene O'Neill, who started his dramatic career after the World War I, has directed his attention to investigate the nature of a strictly American brand of illusion and its clash with social reality. The image of success-chiefly success in money-making in America today, dominated by speed, specialization, mass advertisement, standardized ideals and entertainments, giant monopoly and excitement — has become a necessity for the self respecting man. Illusion, however, has a very different meaning to Eugene O'Neill. On this stage, it takes the shape of dark, gloomy, uncontrollable forces that make sport of man's life. He has a tragic view of "illusion" which causes suffering and shock to its victim. O'Neill's plays are replete with the theme of isolation and loneliness permeating family and social relationships. The concept of isolation and loneliness is vividly illustrated by the title of David Riesman's sociological treatise, *The Lonely Crowd*,[4] and is comprehensively analysed in Jung's *Modern Man in Search of a Soul*.[5] Riesman demonstrates that in a lonely crowd the individuals are estranged from one another, and communication and mutual understanding are replaced by estrangement and hostility. Jung advances the thesis that science, knowledge, reason, civilization and material progress only do violence to the natural forces which in turn seeks revenge, causing crisis and upheavals. Paul Tillich writes : "Mankind is in the state of universal existential estrangement."[6] The situation is one of all-encompassing isolation and loneliness of mankind.

The existentialist movement actually arose in revolution against the corruption of values in capitalist society. Its basic conviction is that the evils are rooted in the very concept and existence of society. It rejects the view of human being as a social animal growing, enriching himself and realising his freedom in his social relations with others. Therefore, evil is ascribed to science, the accumulation of knowledge, the exploration of reality, the study of economics and history, the extension of democracy and the devotion to reason — all the tools of progress that have been collectively forged by society. Man has to renounce them in order to concentrate on the essential question of "existence."

If Eugene O'Neill had been a philosopher, instead of being a literary figure, he too, would, perhaps, have come up with ideas very similar to those of the existentialist philosophers. But he chose literature as the vehicle for his views on matters of fundamental importance. Sartre, Camus, Dostoevsky and many other thinkers had found that philosophy was not always the right medium for expressing deep thoughts about so illusive a thing as human soul. That is why, they chose the medium of fiction to express their ideas indirectly. No wonder Unamuno insists that a philosopher is to be a poet as well, and this is the reason why the American playwrights — O'Neill Miller, Tenessee Williams and Edward Albee — chose dramas to express their attitude towards contemporary man and his crisis.

O'Neill was the first American playwright to rival the great European dramatists. His works took American theatre out of its infancy, and at once endowed it with strength and majesty. He is primarily a dramatist of ideas. He was preoccupied with the major concerns of human life and destiny, and man's quest for a meaning in life and his unceasing groping into 'self.' In doing this, he was leading a revolution in American drama. Search for human values has been the main concern of O'Neill, and he reveals his understanding of human situation, human existence and the destiny of man. By pointing to the helplessness of modern man, he also describes in dramatic terms, the goals of man and his values, and the consequent adjustment of the modes of human self. His plays seem to be apparently the dramatization of man's indignation against the universe. But a close scrutiny of them reveals a subtle and unmistakable affirmation of the self and universe. We can say that his plays attempt to illuminate as well as reflect the condition and predicament of man in existentialist terms, revealing the areas of darkness and tension in modern man's consciousness. He believes that man suffers from the sense of alienation in this world; he finds himself completely isolated in a spiritually sterile universe and, therefore, he cannot have a sense of harmony. In his search for identity and his need to belong, man feels his 'lostness' intensely. His works reveal a keen sense of loss of connection — of connection with God, nature, society, family. The tensions in his works are connected merely with the struggle against alienation. It is evident from his plays that a man has to face stiff time in a world without God, without love and without trust in life. He presents an existentialist's view of life, and so existential problems are very frequently dramatized in his works. It is the turmoil of a whole generation that finds its artistic presentation in his plays. He depicts in a very systematic and convincing manner the depth of human anxiety, despair, emptiness and willinglessness.

Friederich Nietzsche exercised tremendous impact on O'Neill's mind, and had gone a long way in shaping his intellectual sensibility. O'Neill follows him in his affirmation of life, and stresses the need for living a purposeful life and not for the sake of eternity. But he differs from Nietzsche in his concept of God, and refuses to believe that "God is dead." He is interested in the relationship between man and God, and has a monistic vision of the universe, with God and man as parts of its unity. He has openly criticised the commercial civilization for making man spiritually bankrupt.

Arguably, O'Neill can be regarded as an existentialist humanist in his own right. His inquiry into the nature of human condition is made in the existentialist mode. The recurring themes in his plays — *viz.*, man alienated from an absurd world and the individual estranged from society; the individual's isolation and subjectivity; his consequent feelings of anxiety, anguish, despair and nausea; the individual facing his own nothingness, or confronting his guilt; and his assertion of personal freedom through irrevocable choice, particularly in extreme suitations — show his pre-occupation with the existentialist element. His main interest in his plays is the targedy of the individual in the society of the present times.

True, O'Neill present a stark, existential picture of life, and existential problems are frequently dramatized in his works. It is the turmoil of a whole generation that finds its artistic presentation in his plays. He studies man in his immediate situation or context and the way it affects man's life. He depicts in a convincing manner the depth of human anxiety and despair about fate and death, emptiness, meaninglessness, etc. He dramatizes the feelings anguish, guilt and despair which are the direct outcome of modern man's search for self-hood and belongingness in this hostile world. *The Emperor Jones* is an example of the lost self and of the confusion, dread, guilt and despair Jones experiences when forced to confront the real world. The *Strange Interlude* is concerned with the anguish of everyman. The bums in Harry Hope's Saloon in *The Iceman Cometh* suffer from alienation, and have desire to communicate with the outside world. *Hughie* presents a paralysed view of life, of modern man's existential situation in which under-developed characters find themselves misfits in an overdeveloped society. The characters live in isolation, and have no desire to come in touch with others. The play finally shows that the essence of human existence lies in human interdependence, and in the transformation of isolation into communication and bitterness into love. *More Stately Mansions* deals with the theme of man's universal prostitution and utter lack of humanity. The play shows modern man's degeneration in the moral scale, and his readiness to sell himself to get petty ends.

There is a constant tension between the real and the ideal in O'Neill's plays. Illusions incapacitate a man for meaningful action, and yet without them life becomes unbearable. Dreams are a powerful means of denying or overlooking the harsh realities of life. Illusions make us see things in their true prespective. Illusion and reality are not opposed to each other in O'Neill's plays. A stage-illusion ultimately becomes a life-reality. He is never in favour of running away from life, but impresses upon us that life must be faced in a bold and heroic manner. Dreams are indispensable, and they sustain our interest in life. Illusion and reality together make life. Reality often becomes so unbearable that one should have one illusion or the other to make life livable. Illusions are destructive, but they are also necessary. The bums in *The Iceman Cometh* do not feel the need to distinguish between reality and illusion, and so for them illusion is reality. Paradoxically, their illusions are the only reality for them.

Illusions can also be very dangerous and destructive, if they are nourished in excess. Such illusions are likely to disturb human relations, and can lead to misunderstanding and confusion. O'Neill's too much preoccupation with illusions has let the critics point out that there is a ring of pessimism in his plays. They say that the picture of life in his plays is bleak and pessimistic. However, such views of critics are unjustified, and it can be stated that O'Neill's pessimism is of a man in this world in which he must live and justify himself, if life is to have a meaning. His pessimism is born of man, not of God or the universe. He looks at the worst only to suggest a way out of the evils of the contemporary society. His is not an unrelieved pessimism. In his philosophy, man's predicament is of his own making and an amelioration of his lot is possible. He is a "pessimistic optimist," and always hopes for the best. His contention is that a work of art is always happy, as it aims at discovering the truth and helps us in getting rid of illusions. His affirmative philosophy of life is not a withdrawal from, but a call back to, life. He strikes a characteristic note of affirmation, of faith in man and God, and of joy in living. His heroes show hope even in the forces of evil and destruction; rather they keep up their attitude of defiance against them.

The present work aims at exploring the theme of isolation and loneliness in the major plays of Eugene O'Neill, written during the three phases of his career as a dramatist. It is, therefore, devoted to study the plays of Eugene O'Neill in their chronological sequence in the chapters that follow. The theme of isolation and loneliness has been brought out by analysing the plays in respect of their plot, characters, situations, dialogue and the stylistic devices adopted by the dramatist.

REFERENCES

[1] Barrett H. Clark, *Eugene O'Neill : The Man and His Plays* (New York : Dover, 1947), p. 152.

[2] Quoted in K.F. Reinhardt, *The Existentialist Revolt* (New York : Ungar, 1960), p. 27.

[3] Kierkegaard, *Fear and Trembling and the Sickness on the Death* (Garden City, N.Y. : Doubleday, 1954), p. 168.

[4] David Riesman, *The Lonely Crowd* (New Haven : Yale University Press, 1961).

[5] C.G. Jung, *Modern Man in Search of a Soul* (N.Y. : Harcourt, Brace, 1953).

[6] Paul Tillich, "Existential Analysis and Religious Symbols" *Four Existentialist Theologians*, ed. Herberg (Gardencity, N.Y. : Doubleday, 1958), p. 285.

2

The Early Phase

This chapter presents an analysis of the four full-length plays of Eugene O'Neill, written in the early part of his dramatic career. They are *Beyond the Horizon* (1918), *The Emperor Jones* (1920), *The Hairy Ape* (1921), and *All God's Chillun Got Wings* (1923). The successful dramatization of these plays established O'Neill as one of the greatest playwrights of the time. In them, he brilliantly expresses man's tragic agony in a helpless world. They show how man suffers from a sense of loneliness and isolation which arises out of insecurity and social evils, and how his unending struggle for the search of belongingness leaves him in an isolated state.

Out of the four plays, discussed here, the last three deal with the racial prejudices and the protagonists of these plays belong to the black race. The chief characters in them suffer from the loss of belongingness which ironically they find in their deaths. In comparison to the female characters, the males in these plays suffer more deeply. The women are selfish, non-cooperative and are the cause behind the tragic suffering of men. So far as the dramatic technique is concerned, through the use of expressionistic symbolism, O'Neill delineates the tragedy of men's isolation and loneliness at different levels.

1. *BEYOND THE HORIZON* (1918)

Beyond the Horizon, the first major play written by Eugene O'Neill, established his reputation as a playwright by winning the first Pulitzer Prize for him. As his first full-length play, it is naturally built upon all his significant earlier works. About it Arthur and Barbara Gelb remark : "O'Neill expressed for the first time on a large scale his 'hopeless hope' philosophy, painting with sweep and grandeur the tragic theme that was soon to distinguish him from all American playwrights who had come before."[1] It deals with his sense of special relationship between man and his environment. The play depicts the tragic story of Robert Mayo, the true tragic protagonist who has lost his harmony with the environment. Owing to this loss of harmony, he is unable to belong to his circumstances, and so suffers from a sense of isolation throughout his life. His loss of belongingness, and the conflict between his dream and desire compel him to live between hope's eternal optimism and the inevitability of despair. Ultimately, he remains an alienated person till the end of his life.

The play mainly deals with the tragic story of two brothers, Robert and Andrew, who are in love with the same girl, Ruth. Both the brothers are opposite to each other in nature, and in their approach towards life. Robert is a young farmborn dreamer, whose romantic mind and frail body yearn for the open sea, the swarming ports of the mysterious East, and the beckoning world beyond the line of hills which enclose his native town. On the other hand, Andrew has no interest in all sorts of romantic imagination. He is a 'real Mayo,' a true son of the soil, born to do nothing but work in the field. The play begins with the incident that Robert is about to ship on a voyage with his uncle. His brother, who is happy with the farm, is looking forward to his marriage with Ruth Atkins, his childhood sweet-heart. When Robert tells Ruth that he loves her, her response causes him to abandon his chance of escape and to marry Ruth, while Andrew replaces his brother on the sea voyage. Robert proves inept and temperamentally unsuited to farming, and brings the farm to slow disintegration and ruin. He realises that his wife, who has become resentful and morose, has always loved his brother. Anyhow, they have managed to pass their time for the sake of their daughter and mother. But after the death of his mother and the baby, Robert becomes more helpless and faces a lot of economic trouble. Then, Andrew returns, successful and wealthy, and finds Robert surrounded by the ruins he has created and dying of tuberculosis. On his death-bed, Robert still dreams of freedom beyond the horizon and of reconciliation between Ruth and Andrew.

The play opens with the description of a countryyard atmosphere, which projects the inner life of the characters :

> The road runs diagonally from the left, forward, to the right, rear, and can be seen in the distance winding toward horizon like a pale ribbon between the low, rolling hills with their freshly-ploughed fields clearly divided from each other.[2]

This suggests the separateness of Andrew and Robert : "A straggling line of piled rocks, too low to be called a wall, separates this field from the road" (p. 5), again, symbolised the attitude of the two brothers towards life. The field stands for Andrew, the elder brother who believes in work, and the road is indicative of the day-dreamer Robert who aspires what lies beyond. On account of their own nature, they are separated from each other by a wall of piled rocks which are symbolic of the naked realities of life.

At first we find Robert sitting on the fence, reading a book in the beauteous atmosphere of the fading sun. His appearance expresses his personality : "There is a touch of the poet about him expressed in his high forehead and wide, dark eyes. His features are delicate and refined leaning to weakness in the mouth and chin" (p. 6). This individuality of his character keeps him apart from the rest of the characters in the play. It seems that he is haunted by a sense of isolation which ensues from his romantic nature ever in search of beauty. O'Neill describes him thus : "... he turns his head toward the horizon, gazing out over the fields and hills. His lips move as if he were reciting something to himself" (p. 6). On the other hand, Andrew is returning from his work in the field, "an opposite type of Robert — husky, sunbronzed, handsome in a large-featured, manly fashion — a son of the soil, intelligent in a shrewd way, but with nothing of the intellectual about him" (p. 6). This shows his devotion towards work in contrast to Robert's worship of beauty. Both the brothers are sharply distinguished by their thoughts. Being a farmer's son, whose duty is to work in the field, Robert's expectation lies beyond the horizon. His high ambition is the cause of his loneliness, which compels him to seek some peace in a lonely atmosphere, for which he is isolated from his family.

Their discussion reveals the fact that Robert is about to go on a sea voyage to the beautiful foreign world beyond the horizon with his uncle, Captain Dick Scott. As he is not satisfied with the environment to which he belongs, he says to Andrew : "What I want to do now is keep on moving, so that I won't take root in any one place" (p. 9). It clearly shows that he has lost his roots, his identity; and his motive behind the voyage is nothing but his search for identity. He thinks that his search for identity may be fulfilled by his urge for beauty. He describes the cause behind his journey to Andrew :

> Supposing I was to tell you that it's just beauty that's calling me, the beauty of the far off and unknown, the mystery and spell of the East, which lures me in the books I've read, the need of the freedom of great wide spaces, the joy of wandering on and on — in quest of the secret which is hidden just over there, beyond the Horizon? Suppose I told you that was the one and only reason for my going? (p. 18).

Robert's longing for beauty is marred by the confession of Ruth. On the eve of his departure, he comes to know that he is being loved by Ruth, who, he thought, loved Andrew. For the sake of Ruth, he changes his plan :

> Ruth told me this evening that — she loved me. It was after I'd confessed I loved her. I told her I hadn't been conscious of my love until after the trip had been arranged, and I realized it would mean — leaving her. That was the truth. I didn't know until then... I hadn't intended telling her anything but — suddenly — I felt I must. I didn't think it would matter, because I was going away, and before I came back I was sure she'd have forgotten. And I thought she loved-some one else... And then she cried and said it was I she'd loved all the time, but I hadn't seen it (Simply). So we're going to be married — very soon — and I'm happy — and that's all there is to say (Appealingly). But you see, I couldn't go away now-even if I wanted to (p. 46).

At first, Robert insists Ruth to accompany him in his voyage. But she refuses, citing the reason of her mother Mrs. Atkin's illness and her own outlook on life. She says to Robert :

> I wouldn't want to live in any of those outlandish places you were going to. I couldn't stand it there, I know I couldn't — not knowing anyone. It makes me afraid just to think of it. I've never been away from here, hardly and — I'm just a home body. I'm afraid (p. 30).

Her bent of mind is entirely practical, contrary to the poetical mind of Robert. In fact, she is trapped in the cage of illusion — she hopes she will lead a life of conciliation with Robert. But the nature of Robert is incompatible with hers. Robert is a man living in the world of imagination, *i.e.*, poetry, and she, for this transitory charm, wooes him.

In order to satisfy Ruth and to marry her, he chooses the

wrong way and decides to stay at home instead of leaving. Now he begins to think that perhaps he may be able to find all his dreams and desires in his life with Ruth. Robert says :

> I could find all the things I was seeking for here, at home on the farm. The mystery and the wonder — our love should bring them home too, I think love must have been the secret — the secret that called to me from over the world's rim — the secret beyond every horizon; and when I did not come, it came to me ... Oh, Ruth, you are right; Our love is sweeter than any distant dream (p. 31).

Robert's changing of decision astonishes the members of his family because farming is entirely different to his nature. His father does not like his idea, but with all his confidence Robert tries to convince him : "I'm going to settle right down and take a real interest in the farm, and do my share. I'll prove to you, Pa, that I'm as good a Mayo as you are — or Andy, when I want to be" (p. 49). Although his confidence is completely based on his false idea, he again goes on saying :

> I know what you're going to say, and that's another false idea you've got to get out of your heads. It's ridiculous for you to persist in looking on me as an invalid. I'm as well as anyone, and I'll prove it to you if you'll give me half a chance. Once I get the hang of it, I'll be able to do as hard a day's work as anyone. You wait and see (p. 50).

Therefore, Robert remains behind in marrying Ruth, feeling that love is perhaps what he hoped to find in his search.

By knowing the decision of Robert, Andrew suddenly decides to take the place of his brother and this is another matter of surprise for everyone. He does so because he himself had loved Ruth and he was expecting to marry her. He is anguished. In order to release his anguish and not to become an obstacle between his beloved and his brother, he leaves for the sea voyage — the world of dreams where he can mitigate the pain of his heart. From this point, he wants to be alienated, to be away from the rest of the world. His father James Mayo warns him against the wrong decision :

> Your place is right here on this farm — the place you was born to by nature — and you can't tell me no different. I've watched you grow up, and I know your ways, and they're my ways. You're running' against your own nature, and you're goin'to be a 'mighty sorry fir it if you do (p. 58).

Despite the warning of his father, Andrew sails in place of his brother in order to forget Ruth. He confesses the reason of his leaving to his brother : "But you can't expect me to stay around here and watch you two together, day after day — and me alone" (p. 44). Andrew's decision of leaving the farm is nothing but a way of escapism. He does not want to witness the happy life of the couple, and suffer alone in the farm.

After his departure, Robert hopefully accepts his new position as a family man and farmer. Arthur and Barbara Gelb remark :

> Robert makes the mistake of declaring his love for Ruth and staying with her on the farm, instead of following the sea as he had planned. Thus, by winning he loses .... Andrew who having lost Ruth, takes Robert's place as a sailor. But it was pure art that enabled O'Neill to alter an unresolved personal situation into one in which the poet wins the girl while losing his soul and the adventurer grows materialistic in the face of poetic experience he cannot appreciate.[3]

Both the brothers change their ways and are finally separated from each other.

Shortly after the marriage, the reality falls upon romance. The false fabric, which has covered both Ruth and Robert, begins to break and they are now to face the pangs of the bitter realities of life. The setting of Act II becomes quite different from that of the first. The room is no longer set in order. The details in interior setting evoke the image of decay : "The room has changed .... The chairs appear shabby from lack of paint; the table cover is spotted and askew; holes show in the curtains; a child's doll, with one arm gone, lies under the table; a hoe stands in a corner; a man's coat is flung on the couch in the rear; the desk is cluttered up with odds and ends; a number of books are piled carelessly on the side board" (p. 71). It symbolises the change from prosperity to disintegration in the family and characters. The chaos of the room symbolises the chaos in the lives of the characters, especially Robert and Ruth.

Robert is proved as a misfit to the environment. Still he tries his best to manage the farm for the sake of his child and wife. But there occurs a strange change in the character of Ruth. She becomes peevish, and is indifferent towards Robert. One day she even tells him that she did not love him. She loved Andrew, but the momentary charms of Robert made her to say that she loved him :

> What do you think — living with a man like you — having to suffer all the time because you've never been man enough to work and do things like other people. But no! You never own up to that. You think you're so much better than other folks, with your college education, where you never learned a thing, and always reading your stupid books instead of working. I s'pose you think I ought to be *proud* to be your wife — a poor, ignorant thing like me! (Fiercely) But I'm not. I hate it! I hate the sight of you; Oh, if I'd only known! If I hadn't been such a fool to listen to you cheap, silly, poetry talk that you learned out

> of books! If I could have seen how you were in your true self — like you are now — I'd have killed myself before I'd have married you! I was sorry for it before we'd been together a month. I knew what you were really like — when it was too late (pp. 97-98).

Hearing this, all the remaining hopes of Robert are shattered. From the very beginning, Ruth is a practical woman whose only aspiration is to lead a happy life with Robert. It becomes difficult for her to suppress her desires. She becomes more outspoken day by day. He also realises his mistake, and says : "... And now — I'm finding out what you're really like — what a — a creature I've been living with. (*With a harsh laugh*) God! It wasn't that I've kept on telling myself that I must be wrong — like of fool! — like a damned fool" (p. 98).

The relation between Ruth and Robert becomes more polluted day by day. The reality tortures both so terribly that they are from this moment completely alienated from each other. The remaining hopes of their union are lost. Neither Robert nor she finds any meaning in life except the love of their child, for whose sake they continue to live together. They have reached the point from where there is no return. Both, in anguish, lay open their hearts to each other. Robert calls Ruth a 'slut' and she cries 'Andy' Andy.' But Robert, because of his romantic nature, absorbs this shock, and he reticently takes the decision about fulfilling her desire. He is able to do so because he may live a dejected life on account of his very nature of living in the world of dreams. In the meantime, Andy arrives and the curtain falls, ending the First Scene of Act II.

The setting of the Scene II, like the other early settings, is also symbolic. The hot and cloudless day signifies the breaking of illusion and disturbance of mental peace. The bleached, sun-scorched grass symbolies the withering of the illusion of Robert by the sun of truth. We see, "Robert is discovered sitting on the boulder, his chin resting on his hands, staring out toward the horizon seaward. His face is pale and haggard, his expression one of utter despondency" (p. 101). The alteration between the spacious and cramped sets illustrates the conflicting desires of the two brothers, Robert and Andrew. The details in the outdoor setting suggest movement and distance which express Robert's dream for the 'beyond.' We find Mary, his daughter, playing beside him and insisting him to play with her, but he shows no keenness. He is indifferent to her because she is the symbol of his withered love with Ruth :

MARY : (*Pulling at his hand solicitously*). Is Dada sick?

ROBERT : (*looking at her with a forced smile*) No, dear, why?

ROBERT : (gently). No, dear, not today. Dada doesn't feel like playing today (p. 101).

Robert, disgusted with life, sits in the farm when Andrew comes. Robert has again acquired his previous temperament. He again wants to absorb himself in the dream world where he can forget his mental and physical agony. Inevitably, he gets close to his past, and cannot live alienated from his past. We mark that by marrying Ruth, who is forgetful about her past, all sorts of sufferings surround him because he is severed from his very nature.

On the other hand, his brother Andrew is no more happy with his sea voyage. He travels through a number of places, some of which like Argentina, where he has business opportunity, are of his interest. Although he has travelled a lot, he does not find any pleasure in the sea. He says to Robert :

> Had to do something or I'd gone mad. The days were like years. Nothing to look at but sea and sky. No place to go. A regular prison. (*He laughs*) And as for the East you used to rave about-well.

> you ought to see it, and smell it; and the chinks and Japs and Hindus and the rest of them -- you can have them; One walk down one of their filthy narrow streets with the tropic sun beating on it would sicken you for life with the "wonder and mystery" you used to dream of. I can say one thing for it through — it certainly has the stink market cornered (pp. 109-10).

Basically, Andrew is a farmer, a son of the soil, and feels happy only over the land. It shows that both the brothers are sharply opposite to each other in their nature on account of which they are alienated form themselves. If Andrew had stayed at home and Robert had gone to sea, each would have held true to his essential nature and been able to live in harmony with the elements of his environment. For, Robert belongs to sea and Andrew to the land. By changing their paths, both have lost their sense of belongingness to their surroundings. Robert, in the cup of the hills, cut off from the horizon, is imprisoned forcibly and held back from joining the elements to which he really belongs. His weakness and his romanticism are irrelevant; until he can unite himself with the sea, he can not be strong. On land, the unyielding furrows are sterile, and likewise Andrew does not find any interest in voyage but travels unmoved to charming shores, seeing only abused land.

Ruth now gets diverted from Robert and is attracted to Andrew. She starts talking to Andrew in the same way as she talked to Robert before their marriage. She is the root cause behind the tragedy of both the brothers. She has repeated the history set by beautiful women. O'Neill describes her in these words :

> She is a healthy, blonde, out-of-door girl of twenty, with a graceful, slender figure. Her face, though inclined to roundness, is undeniably pretty, its large eyes of a deep blue set off strikingly by the

> sunbronzed complexion. Her small, regular features are marked by a certain strength — an underlaying, stubborn fixity of purpose hidden in the frankly appealing charms of her fresh youthfulness (pp. 20-1).

As men are very insecure creatures, they certainly need a lot of love and need beautiful women. But unfortunately beautiful women are seldom able to provide love. Love is eternal, an essential, in every human being, but Ruth's conception of love is entirely based on her self-interest. The real intention behind her approach to Andrew is nothing but only security. Living a hopeless life with Robert, she becomes helpless and insecure, at least economically. Therefore, in order to get security she insists Andrew to stay in the farm. She says :

> .... Oh, Andy, you can't go! Why we've all thought — we've all been hoping and praying you was coming home to stay, to settle down on the farm and see to things. You mustn't go ... — and how the farm'll be ruined if you leave it to Rob to look after. You can see that (pp. 120-21).

But by now Andrew has no more interest in her. He, like others, is passing his life in solitude. He is also the victim of the same disease of isolation which has affected Ruth and Robert. He has borne the pain of separation to such an extent as he no more longs for the union. He is dejected : "Everybody hereabouts seems to be on edge today. I begin to feel as if I'm not wanted around" (p. 125). That is why, he prepares himself again for the sea voyage.

The first scene of the third act begins with the description of the interior setting, the sitting-room of the farm house. It is somewhat similar to the first scene of the second act. This alteration between indoor and outdoor setting has a greater significance in the life of Robert. The indoor scenes, which are cooped in a small room, evoke his imprisonment. The outdoor settings are correlated with the actions of the character.

The relationships among the characters are, more or less, the same. But physicallv Ruth as well as Robert is deteriorated. O'Neill describes their physical conditions thus :

> She (Ruth) has aged horribly. Her pale, deeply lined face has the stony lack of expression of one to whom nothing more can ever happen, whose capacity for emotion has been exhausted. When she speaks, her voice is without timbre, low and monotonous ..... His (Robert's) hair is long and unkempt, his face and body emaciated. There are bright patches of crimson over his cheek-bones and his eyes are burning with fever (p. 132).

Robert has been the victim of tuberculosis, and his nature has become peevish. Though apparently he says that he is quite healthy, yet actually he is approaching, gradually towards the death. Both he and Ruth are isolated form each other to an extent which cannot be compensated by any other means. He desperately kisses her. The intensity of the pain of separation is reflected here : "... one kiss — the first in years, isn't it?" (p. 141), and it reveals that there has hardly existed any relation between them for give some years.

Robert's condition worsens continuously; he slowly moves towards his end. In the meantime, Andrew returns from his voyage with a doctor for Robert. The doctor also feels that the things have gone worst, and only some miracle can save Robert. Andrew, because of his optimistic nature, believes in miracle, but Robert is devoid of any hope, any positive attitude towards life.

In Ruth, there is a great conflict between her inner and outer selves. She did not marry Andrew; instead, she chose Robert. But now she realises that she had committed a mistake. That is why, she again loves Andrew. Her conflicting attitudes separate her from others as well as from her own self. Though with someone, she is alone. She says : "I did't want to be alone with him that way" (p. 143), and she answers to Andrew about her relation with Robert :

> ANDREW : And you've lived together for five years with this horrible secret between you?
>
> RUTH : We've lived in the same house — not as a man and wife (p. 168).

Her answer clearly shows that she is divided within herself. Neither she belongs to her husband nor she entirely belongs to herself for which she suffers from a sense of insecurity and loneliness.

Robert now is no more interested in his life. His disease is not terrible, still he does not try to save his life. Haunted by the sense of aloneness, he still wishes to witness the sight of horizon. He orders Andrew : ".... Pull the bed around so it'll face the window, will you, Andy? I can't sleep, but I'll rest and forget if I can watch the rim of the hills and dream of what is waiting beyond .... And the shut door, Andy. I want to be alone" (p. 164). He would better like to go beyond the horizon, *i.e.*, beyond any illusion, any falsity, which is possible only after death. He thinks that death will break the wall of isolation between Ruth and Andrew. He takes a promise from Andrew of marrying Ruth after his death.

In the last moment, Robert's attempt to re-establish a vision parallels the manner in which his early dream originated.

He says :

> ... Don't you see I'm happy at last-because I'm making a start to the far-off places — free — free; freed from the farm-free to wander on and on-eternally; Even the hills are powerless to shut me in now ... Look; Isn't it beautiful beyond the hills? I can hear the old voices calling me to come ... And this time I'm going — I'm free; It isn't the end. It's a free beginning — the start of my voyage; Don't you see? I've won to my trip-

> the right of release-beyond the horizon; Oh, you ought to be glad-glad for my sake; ... Andy; .... Remember Ruth — (p. 173).

He dies, but his sacrifice will not fulfil his hopes because the realities with which Ruth and Andrew have been acquainted will ever stand between them, and they will never be able to establish any real contact, and therein lies the tragedy of Robert's life. Apropos of this Doris V. Falk rightly remarks : "Robert's death is an escape, not a victory. It is a sorry compensation for a barren life, wasted in a futile search for identity."[4] By losing their identity, their sense of belongingness, all the three major characters have failed to establish the real communion among themselves and have remained alienated from one another as well as from their environment.

2. *THE EMPEROR JONES* (1920)

The Emperor Jones is O'Neill's much talked-about play. In this drama, there is an eternal conflict with those powers which are beyond man's control. Man is represented in relation with God. As the playwright opines, "most modern plays are concerned with the relation between man and man, but that does not interest me at all. I am interested only in the relation between man and God."[5] Man's lack of faith in some supreme power and his too much materialism and inner emptiness are the cause of his tragic fate. This has always been the main subject for drama because :

> as far as we can judge, man is much the same creature, with the same primal emotions and ambitions and motives, the same powers and the same weaknesses, as in the time when the Aryan race started toward Europe from the slopes of the Himalayas. He has become better acquainted with those powers and those weaknesses, and he is learning ever so slowly not to control them.[6]

Ultimately, it leads to isolate him from his environment as well as from his inner being. He reaches a position where he finds himself alone and insecure, and becomes an isolated being. Sometimes his overambitiousness, his false confidence and self-pride leave him in an isolated state. This happens in the case Brutus Jones, the protagonist of *The Emperor Jones*.

The play deals with the rise and fall of Brutus Jones, the negro and fugitive emperor, who reminds us of the Shakespearean tragic hero Macbeth. In this connection, Julius Bab remarks :

> This Negro is only an insolent tyrant in a Caribbean island; yet the collapse of his criminal egomania, the defeat of his extraordinary vitality by the imaginings of his own brain — these are represented so magnificently, so movingly, that the play seems to me to offer a complete parallel with Shakespear's Macbeth.[7]

Jones, an ex-pullman porter, through deception and corruption, becomes the emperor and possessor of great wealth on an island in the West Indies. After achieving this his life-style and his ways of thinking begin to change. He tries to ignore the reality and his own past. He is involved in clash with one of his friends while playing the games of dice, which results in his murdering of his friend. This sends him to prison. But in the prison he also kills the guards and again becomes a convict. In order to save himself, he flees away and reaches an island. Because he is a tricky fellow, he impresses the innocent natives of that island and becomes the ruler of that region. Since by heart he is incompatible with the negro people, he exercises pressure over them. He imposes extra-taxes and other duties which are unendurable for the subjects. He earns a lot of money and deposits it in a foreign bank as well as keeps it secretly under the white rocks in the Jungle. He does so because he always suffers from a sense of insecurity. His life is restless, and he cannot share his feelings with the negro people, who belong to his own class.

Obviously, Jones is isolated from that class of people to which he himself belongs. Outwardly, he is very ambitious and determined. But inwardly, he is always haunted by a sense of unknown fear and loss of security. To save himself from the fury of his people, he also beguiles them saying that he can only be killed by a silver bullet, spreading superstition among them. His brutish activities make the people conscious of their own sufferings and make them rebel against him. Jones, in order to save himself, again decides to take flight and starts off philosophically the lonely march that takes him to Martinique, the world where, he thinks, wealth and freedom await him. He has hidden food in the forest and his revolver is loaded with five lead bullets meant for his enemies, and a silver bullet for himself in case he is ever really cornered.

But in the forest he does not find his secretly kept belongings. Like a mad person, he removes the white rocks in the forest, but is unable to locate the place. He shows vain courage, hope and smartness. His body cannot keep balance with his mind. However, night falls, and to the incessant accompaniment of pounding drums he conforms to the dark faces of his own mind and the history of his own race. In a terrifying series of short episodes, he is assailed by the phantoms of his victims and his past life, journeying back through auction block and slave ship to his primer origins in the Congo. Out of fear, he has fired all the bullets of his pistol at the images which pass before his sight. At dawn, the natives, led by Lem, start their search and find Jones laying very near the place where he had entered the forest. They fire a silver bullet into his body, believing it the only means to end his life as he had told them.

From the outset, Jones leads a different life. We find him an entirely isolated person. He had neither any family nor any kith and kin. He has no interest to run his life in a joint way. We come to know all these facts about his past life from his conversation with the cockney trader, Henery Smithers, his partner through whom he has earned a lot of money. His discussion with Smithers shows that he is aware of the consequences of his deeds. That is why, he has deposited all his money in a foreign bank. He starts his life in a negative way, involves in gambling, killing and all sorts of anti-social activities. After killing the prison guards in the United States, he comes to this island. By nature he is shrewd and suspicious, and this keeps him away from his surroundings. About his appearance and nature, the playwright says :

> He is tall, powerfully-built, full-blooded negro of middle age. His features are typically negroid, yet there is something decidedly distinctive about his face — an underlying strength of will, a hardly self-reliant confidence in himself that inspires respect. His eyes are alive with a keen, cunning intelligence. In manner he is shrewd, suspicious, evasive....[8]

His manners and appearance make him a different being and because of his own nature he is cut-off from the society. Neither in the States nor in West Indian island, he has established any social links with anybody which is a natural instinct in every social being. Identity is nothing but a farce for him. Being a convict, he becomes a ruler at the cost of his identity. But the identity which he assumes in the island becomes false because he has again done the same mistake. It seems that treachery is part and parcel of his nature. He always faces the problem of identity. But whenever he gets a new identity by his tricky efforts, he misuses it. Being a negro, he hates the negros like anything, and thus he never tries to identify himself with his own class to which he really belongs. When he leaves for the forest, he says to Smithers :

> Does you think I'd slink out de back door like a common nigger? And de Emperor Jones leaves de way he comes, and that black trash don't dare stop him — not yet .... (p. 16).

He never considers himself a negro; rather he thinks that the black people of his race are inferior to him. It clearly shows that he has no sense of fellow-feeling. Time and again, he calls "nigger," "bloody niger," which indicates that he has no sense of brotherhood and belongingness. Always he is haunted by a sense of isolation; he belongs neither to himself nor to his own classes of people. Even he has not a sense of respect for the white people. While Smithers warns him of the danger he has to face in wild forest, he calls him :

> Look — a — heat white man; Does you think
> I'su a natural bo-n-fool? (p. 13).

This shows his false confidence and egoism which keep him isolated from the mass. He hates both the white and black people, and this ultimately separates him from the society. Again, when Smithers reminds him about his early days in the island, he expresses the same :

> Talk polite, white man; Talk polite,
> You heah me; I'm boss heah now, is you
> forgettin'? (pp. 6-7).

But, on the contrary, he has forgotten his own past after attaining the emperorhood.

His oversmartness places him in a lonely state. He is confident that he can make people fool in any circumstances at any time, and says to Smithers :

> Think dese ign'rent bush niggers dat ain't got brain enuff to know deir own names even can catch Brutush Jones? Hah, I s'pects note; Not on yo'life; Why man de white men went after me wid blood hounds where I come from an' I jes'laughs at 'em. It's a shame to fool dese black trash around heah, dey're so easy. You watch me, man. I'll make dem look sick, I will I'll be 'cross de plain to the edge of de forest by time dark come once in de woods in de night, they got a swell chance o' findin' dis baby .... (p. 13).

Jones's false pride and vain courage always make a dividing line between him and his surroundings. None but he himself is responsible for this gap which keeps him aloof from the trend. Neither he considers anybody's suggestion nor he tries to understand the capacity of others. When Smithers reminds him of the obstacle he has to face in jungle and warns him of Lem and his rituals, Jones flatters :

> I ain't no chicken — liver like you is. Trees an 'me, we'se friends, and dar's a full moon comin' bring me light. And let dem po' niggers make all de full spells dey's se a min' to. Does yo's'pect I'se silly enuff to b'lieve in ghosts an'ha'nts an'all dat ole woman's talk? (p. 15).

As soon as Jones enters the forest, he loses his self-confidence; he is haunted by a sense of loneliness. But his proud nature, his egoistical temperament, does not allow him to accept the fear wholeheartedly. He consoles himself to avoid the obstacles which come in his way. The dark night in the forest reveals his true personality, his dual nature. We find a separating line between his mind and his body. He seems to be an abnormal being; his body does not cooperate with his will. He becomes tired, but still shows his vain courage :

> Feet, you is holdin' up yo' end fine an' I sutinly hopes you ain't blisterin' none. It's time you git a rest...You is still in de pink — on'y a little mite faverish. Cool yo' selfs. Remember you done got a long journey yit befo' you.... (p. 18).

In spite of all his false consolation, a sense of fear is already developed within him. He feels hungry and tired, and does not find the 'Box of grub' which he has secretly kept under the white stone. His sense of fear does not allow him to light the match — stick, and he addresses to himself :

> Niger, is you gone crazy mad? Is you lightin' matches to show dem whar you is? (p. 19).

The natives, whom he considers as fools, now begin to frighten him. He wants to hide himself from their sight.

In the next scene he faces the same type of obstacle in his way; he is frightened by the appearance of Jeff whom he murdered before and becomes more nervous. Out of fear he also fires at him and again loses his second bullet. Still he has not lost all his hope to escape from the island. But at the same time his attitude shows that he is aware of the consequence :

> Dey's gettin' near; Dey's comin' fast;
> And heah I is shootin' to let 'em
> know jes' whar I is; Oh, Gorry, I'se
> got to run (p. 22).

With the beginning of the scene IV, his condition becomes pathetic; he, trapped by the wild forest, does not find any proper path to move. The royalty of emperorhood and its costume seem burden for him. Out of anger he says :

> I'm meltin' wid heat; Runnin' an' runnin' an' runnin; Damn' dis heah coat; Like a starit jacket; (He tears off his coat and flings it away from him, revealing himself stripped to the waist) Dere; Dat's better; Now I kin breath .... Dere; I gits rid o'dem fippety Emperor Trappin's an' I travels lighter.... (p. 23).

By throwing the coat and costume he has thrown his emperor's job only to save himself, but he is unable to take himself away from abnormality. He is not able to avoid the sounds of tom-tom. To do away with the natives and the tom-tom, he says :

> I must' 'a' put some distance between myself an'dem — runnin' like dat — and yit — dat damn drum sounds jes'de same — nearer, even. Well, I guess I a'most holds my lead any how. Dey wont' never catch up. If only my fool legs

> stards up. Oh, I'se sorry I evah went in far dis. Dat. Emperor job is sho' hard to shake... (p. 23).

In his roaming in the forest his true personality is revealed through his mental agony. His dual nature keeps him away from himself and makes a wall within his mind. He has been isolated from his self. The sound of the tom-tom contributes a lot to reveal his true personality :

> The tom-tom in *The Emperor Jones* can be compared to the repeated blast of the whistle in *Bound East for Cardiff*; some would call them stage devices to excite the nerves of the audience. In reality they are symbolical elements dramatized; they represent, in both cases, a brooding fate, a predestination...O'Neill is dealing with ancestral ternors latent in the sound, as with Jones, or with a strange, cruel Nature, as in all his sea dramas, man's destiny here always depends on a terrible, unequal struggle between man and a created reality from which he is sharply distinguished.[9]

Ultimately, he turns into a split person. There is a clear distinction between his thought and deed. The sin he has committed in his past life now appears to him and reveals his true personality. But in each instance he commits the same mistake; he fires at the prison guard and at the same time asks for his shovel :

> Whar's my shovel? Gimme my shovel 'til I split his damn head (p. 25).

This shows that his inner being never forgets his past and makes a distinct point between his present and past. He recollects his past, feels he is the same Negro prisoner and again fires at the image of the prison guard.

When a man tries to deny his past, his origin, he gets away from his self. Belongingness becomes a problem for him. That is the tragedy from which Jones is suffering now.

His inner being constantly reminds him of his past, but his will power denies it and makes him busy in his present. His false pride and his indifferent attitude to the people of his own race to which he belongs keeps him away from himself. He does not realise his true identity and ultimately becomes alienated from his own self. As Doris V. Falk explains :

> Jones's hopeless flight through the forest is not from the natives at all, but from himself — the fundamental self from which his blind pride and its self-image have so long separated him, and which, inevitably, comes into its own. This is the primary symbolism of his movement through the forest in a circle, hypnotized by the rhythm of a drum beat and ending where he began. The progress of Jones is progress in self-understanding; it is the stripping off of the masks of self, layer by layer, just as bit by bit his "emperor's" uniform is ripped from his back, until at the end he must confront his destiny — himself — in nakedness.[10]

The ghosts whom Jones meets in the forest are nothing but his past; each represents an aspect of himself or a hidden motive of his past action. It continually haunts him step by step. In the scene in which he confronts the slave auctioner, his condition is more picturesque. He is naked and exhausted, and is surrounded by a group of savages who belong to his own race. He is frightened by seeing the activity of slave auctioner :

> What you all doin,' white folks? What all dis? What you all lookin' at me fo'? What you doin. Wid me, any how... Is dis a auction? is you sellin' me like dey uster befo' de war?...And you sells me? And you buys me? (p. 28).

It clearly shows that Jones begins to realise his own identity, his own self, yet he is to accept it wholeheartedly for which he fires at the auctioner.

Jones becomes desperate after he spends his fifth bullet. He has only the silver bullet with him which he keeps for himself. He realises that he has returned to the clearing where he entered the forest; he is back where his journey began, as if the circular path symbolises his origin. We find him as a convict, and then as an emperor who denies his belongingness to his own race and struggles for a lost security. But finally, he reaches the situation where he finds himself alone. His inner consciousness begins to accept the reality. It becomes impossible on his part to prevent himself from dancing. He joins with the dance of Congo witch-doctor. By that time he forgets about his emperorhood, and he is exhausted and full naked like his ancestors :

> Jones has become completely hypnotized. His voice joins in the incantation, in the cries, he beats time with his hands and sway his body to and fro from the waist. The whole spirit and meaning of the dance has entered into him, has become his spirit. Finally the theme of the pantomime halts on a howl of despair, and is taken up again in a note of savage hope... (p. 32).

In the meantime appears the crocodile God, summoned by the witch-doctor Lem. Jones is frightened by the sight of the crocodile. Suddenly out of fear he remembers his silver bullet, "De silver bullet; You don't git me yit" (p. 32), and he shoots at the crocodile with the silver bullet which he had kept for himself. Thus symbolically he kills his own self.

Jones has no faith in the rituals and the religious ceremonies of the natives. When Smithers warns him of Lem and the rituals of his subjects, he says :

> Dat fool no-count nigger; Does you think I'se scared o'him? I stand him on his thick head more'n once befo' dis, and I does it again if he comes in my way — And dis time I leave him dead nigger fo' sho'... (p. 13).

He has achieved a Whiteman's name and occupation, and has assumed the responsibilities of law, judgment and punishment. Evolving from the primitive, he has become different to his own people and has imposed a new self on himself. By doing so, he has denied the primordial God. His pride, his acts of will, and his conscious individuality as Emperor are the false masks of a white savage. At the end, the black must cast himself upon the God and return home. But by firing the silver bullet he denies to be possessed by God.

Throughout his life he tries to maintain a life of his own, cut off from society, indulged in gambling and killing. Vaguelessly he seeks a new identity, but always finds him insecure. Though lastly he cries for God out of fear and insecurity, yet he refuses God from the beginning. In the first scene when Smithers warns him about the rituals of negro, Jones says :

> Does't you know dey's got to do wid a man was members in good standin'o' de Baptist Church?... It don't git me nothin' to do missionary work for de Baptist Church. I'se after de coin, an' I lays my Jesus on de shelf for de time bein'... (p. 15).

He himself is responsible for his destruction. His over-ambitiousness and his blind pride alienate him from his own self as well as from God and society. But O'Neill provides a heroic death to him. The rebellion shoots him with the silver bullet, which, according to him, is the key to his death, an appropriate symbol of the destruction of self by its own pride and greed. In the end, Smithers rightly remarks about his false royalty :

> Silver bullets; Gawd blimcy, but yer died in the 'eight o' style, any'ow... (p. 35).

The stage technique of the play has added much more to the thematic dimensions of the play. It projects the inner life of the character in a more prominent way. *The Emperor Jones* opens in a spacious high ceilinged farm with bare, white-washed walls, situated on a high ground. It associates grandeur and coldness of heart. The sense of alienation is also evoked and is further enhanced by the selection of the audience-chamber with only the Emperor's throne in it. The white colour predominates because not only the walls are white washed, but even the floor is of white tiles and the portico pillars are also white. The play enacts the search for the real identity of the colored excoriate Jones. He has reached this present state from his humble origin through the white man's trick of business. He is gradually unmasked, and his real black self emerges. The placing of a black man in a context, predominantly white, communicates Jones' sense of guilt and his longing for purity.

In the second scene Jones is seen at the end of the plains where the great forest begins. Only when the eye becomes accustomed to the gloom can the outlines of separate trunks of the nearest tree be made out as enormous pillars of deeper blackness. As his real, black self is exposed, the whiteness deceives. No wonder the white pillars become the enormous pillars of deeper blackness. The forest is the symbol of his unconscious. The play moves through the forest density to open space. The scene shifts successively from the small triangular clearing to the wide dirt road, then to the large circular clearing, and finally to the open space with a single tree. The change is from the closed to the more and more spacious open. This suggests Jones's growing self-recognition.

Sense of belongingness either to a faith or to a feeling has been an inborn quality of man. For his happiness and tranquility, he needs a sense of security and stability. When this age-old belief shatters, he becomes isolated from his being. He considers himself a different person, completely alien to his circumstances. Being isolated from his immediate environment, he feels lonely, alienated and unhappy, and this leads him to seek an identity of his own. When he fails to achieve this lost harmony, he suffers from a sense of isolation.

And thus sense of isolation and loneliness is the major theme in the plays of Eugene O'Neill.

3. *THE HAIRY APE* (1921)

The Hairy Ape, a masterpiece of this celebrated author, also depicts the same theme—isolation or loss of identity and loneliness. Apropos of this play, O'Neill writes :

> *The Hairy Ape* was propaganda in the sense that it was a symbol of man, who has lost his old harmony with nature, the harmony which he used to have as an animal and had not yet acquired in a spiritual way. Thus, not being able to find it on earth nor in heaven, he's in the middle, trying to make peace... Yank can't go forward, and so he tries to go back. This is what his shaking hands with the gorilla meant. But he can't go back to "belonging" either. The gorilla kills him. The subject here is same ancient one that always was and always will be the one subject for drama, and that is man and his struggle with his own fate. The struggle used to be with the gods, but is now with himself, his own past, his attempt "to belong."[11]

In the present context, the title "The Hairy Ape" symbolises the diagnostic character of a savage and ferocious animal in man with an unusal sense of animality. The most remarkable aspect of the dramatist's technique in this play is the blending of the constantly repeated image of the 'ape' with tragic reality. Besides being the central metaphor dominating the whole action of the play, *The Hairy Ape* conveys the image of man's primitiveness and puts forth a living human reality of the present, making us feel like the ape. The artistic fusion of the image and experience heightens the value of the play as a sustained allegory. The strange tyranny is that man is present in a continual repetition of his past. The 'ape' is ingrained in man. He cannot avoid the awaiting doom unless he controls the ape thriving within him.

It seems that the two small words 'hairy' and 'ape' become the root cause of tragedy in the life of the protagonist, Yank. They signify the strength and the brutality in the character of Yank, a distinguished stoker on a transatlantic liner who is proud of his physical strength and superior feelings of belongingness. Yank, a true devotee of work, considers himself as the force behind the moving ship. Dedication to work keeps him aloof from romantic imagination. In reply to his colleague Paddy's song — "Far away in Canada,/Far across the sea,/There's a loss who fondly waits/ Making a home for me—,"[12] Yank, whose only concern is work, says in a bitter voice :

> Shut up, Yuh lousy Boob' where d' yuh get dat tripe? Home? Home, Hell! I'll make a home for yuh! I'll knock yuh dead. Home!! T'hell with home! Where d'yuh get dat tripe? What d'yuh want wit home? (p. 43).

This shows his indifferent attitude towards home or family as supported by Long, his another colleague :

> Listen'ere, Comrades! Yank' are is right.
> "E says this 'ere stinking ship is our 'ome.
> And 'E says as 'ome is 'ell. And 'E 's right! (p. 42).

Ship is everything to them, and they belong to ship. They are so attached to the ship that they hardly think of anything except it; their motto is "Drink, don't think!" (p. 43). Being aloof from the social trend, they are proud of their working capacity, especially Yank, whose confidence in his physical strength and attachment to the ship is superior to that of the rest : "He resembles Brutus Jones in the primitiveness of his nature, but whereas the primitiveness of Jones is spiritual that of Yank is entirely physical. Yank 'belongs' and the world's movement depends upon him; all who do not 'belong' have no interest for him."[13] Comparing himself and his Comrades with the capital class — the ship owners —, Yank rebels : "Dem boids don't amount to nothin'. Dey're just baggage. Who makes dis old tub run? Ain't it us guys? Well den, we belong, don't we? We belong and dey don't. Dat's all" (p. 44).

When old Paddy dreams of the good old days, Yank violently opposes him, considering stockhole a hell :

> Yuh don't belong no more, see.
> Yuh don't get de stuff.
> Yuh're too old (p. 47).

But he is confident and has great faith in his strength and ability. He considers himself the strength behind all power, without whom nothing can run in the man-made, mechanized world. In fact, he considers himself the power behind the moving world :

> I'm de end! I'm de start!... I'm steam and oil for de engines; I'm de ting in noise dat mades yuh hear it; I'm smoke and express trains and steamers and factory whistles; I'm de ting in hold dat makes money! And I'm what makes iron into steel! Steel! dat stands for de whole ting! And I'm steel — steel — steel!... We run de whole woiks. All de rich guys dat tink dey're somep'n dey ain't nothin'! Dey don't belong. But us guys, we're in de move, we're at de bottom, de whole ting is us! (p. 48).

This sense of belongingness and pride in Yank is nothing but his attachment to work. He, at any cost, is ready to prove his belongingness, and this concept of belongingness is entirely built upon his own imagination. He is satisfied with the presents, and is proud of his ability and strength. He asserts that it is his energy on which the ship and the passengers ultimately depend. In reply to Paddy's sentimentality, he boldly affirms : "Tinkin' and dreamin,' what'll that get yuh? What's tinkin' got to do wit it ? We move, don't we? Speed, ain't it? Fog, dat's all you stand for. But we drive trou dat, don't we? We split dat up and smash trou — twenty-five knots a hour! Aw, you, make me sick; Yuh don't belong" (p. 49). Nothing troubles him; he never thinks of God or fate, of home or society. He has no place in his heart for the romantic past of Paddy, nor has any idea to consider the sense of beauty. His only pride is that he 'belongs.'

Yank's encounter with Mildred Dougles, a rich anaemic girl, whose father is the President of the Steel Trust, shakes the whole concept of his belongingness. She is the representative of a world entirely different from that of Yank. She is pale, colourless, decadent and an artificial product of society. Her only aim is to see "how the other half lives" (p. 59). She sees that he is stoke-hole, when he is in full cry. O'Neill describes the reaction as follows :

> He sees MILDRED, like a white apparition in the full light from the open furnace doors. He glares into her eyes, turned to stone. As for her, during his speech she has listened, paralysed with horror, terror, her whole personality crushed, beaten in, collapsed, by the terrific impact of this unknown, abysmal brutality, naked and shameless. As she looks at his gorilla face, as his eyes bore into hers, she utters a low chocking cry and shrinks away from him, putting both hands up before her eyes to shut out the sight of his face, to protect her own. This startles YANK to a reaction. His mouth falls open, his eyes grow bewildered (p. 58).

She never dreamt of seeing such a sequence and a person like Yank. Before leaving the place she exclaims, "Oh, the filthy beast!" (p. 58). But her looks and attitude express much more than what she comments. Yank "feels himself insulted in some unknown fashion in the very heart of his pride" (p. 58). The story here begins to change Yank's life. He becomes confirmed about the look of Mildred when Paddy conveys him : "Sure, 'twas as if she'd seen a great hairy ape escaped from the Zoo!" (p. 62).

This is the greatest blow to Yank's belief as well as to his concept of belongingness. He begins to think that he, who is so proud of his strength, suffers humiliation at the hands of a woman, and the woman who, physically so weak and faint, should have, in turn, appreciated his masculinity. His bodily strength which has claimed superiority although has been identified with the bodily strength of an animal. Body, which has been his only source of pride becomes a prison for him. After that crucial incident he no longer feels that he 'belongs.' Therefore, he tries to escape from the prison where he cannot be content to 'belong.'

The more he thinks about the incident, the more helpless he feels. Finally, he reaches a position where he is described as Rodin's 'Thinker.' It seems as if he is lost within himself, and he has lost something upon which his entire confidence is built on. Gradually, his firm belief is shaken and in order to clear his doubt, he asks : "Say, is that what she called me—a hairy ape?" (p. 63), and again confirms by remembering the incident : "Hairy ape, huh? Sure! Dat's de way she looked at me, aw right. Hairy Ape! So dat's me, huh! (p. 63).

The only thing which has made his life endurable has been his feeling that he belong and is a necessary, vital and human part of social order. But now he starts realising that he is not counted as an individual for anything, and sees the possibility of the restoration of his old self-respect by avenging himself on Mildred. He exclaims :

Ain't she de same as me? Hairy ape, huh?... I'll show her I'm better'n her... I belong and she don't, see! I move and she's dead! Twenty-five knot's a hour, dat's me! (p. 64).

Owing to a faint ray of hope and shattered confidence, Yank, at times, desperately argues of his belongingness; but when he becomes conscious of the reality, his hopes are of no avail and he roars : She don't belong... fix her! Let her come down again and I'll fling her in de furnace! She'll move den! She won't shiver at nothin', den! Speed, dat'll be her! She'll belong den! (p. 64). At the end of this scene, Yank becomes quite violent :

> She done me doit! She done me doit, didn't she? I'll git squire with her! I'll get her some way! Git often me, Youse guys! Lemme up! I'll show her who's a ape! (p. 65).

Yank is now motivated by his strong desire for revenge on Mildred because of whom he has lost his sense of belonging. The immediate problem for him is : Where he stands? If he is not fit for the stoke-hole then where does he fit? He has all along been identified with the ship and the stoke-hole, and when he loses his old identity, the immediate problem for him is to find out a fresh one, as it is the basic nature of each and every individual. His search for a new identity and his urge for belongingness lead him to Fifth Avenue for taking revenge on the upper aristocratic society which Mildred represents.

But the world to which Yank enters is an artificial, materialistic world, a type beyond his knowledge, where people lead a mechanised life. There he also tries desperately to impinge his identity on the so-called upper class society : "Yuh don't belong...I belong.... get me!" (p. 70). Asserting his primitive strength, which has been the cause of his concept of belonging, he says :

> See de steel work? Steel, dats me! Youse guys live on it and tink yuh're somep'n. But I'm in it, see! I'm de hostin' engine dat makes it go up ! I'm it — de inside and bottom of it! Sure! I'm steel and steam and smoke and de rest of it! (p. 70).

What he wants is a recognition. This is not only a problem for Yank, but the problem of the whole social system to which persons like Yank belong. This crisis of identity in American society has closely been studied by Eugene O'Neill. In this connection, Heinrich Straumann remarks : "Viewed in the larger context of nineteenth and twentieth-century writing, this motif grows into one of the three distinct great themes of American literature, viz. the search for identity based on a fundamental feeling of uncertainty about what the individual essentially is and where he belongs... ."[14] His experience in Fifth Avenue makes him aware of his position because this world is far away from the people of his stature. He becomes more helpless than before and this helplessness in a crowded civilized world compels him to seek recognition through his second nature — *i.e.*, violence. Finally, he finds himself in jail after assaulting a person of the so-called upper class.

Earlier, according to him, steel represented steamers, engines, buildings; but now he finds the real steel which symbolises cages, cells, locks, bolts and bars like the dream of every American, which is based on "Liberty! Justice! Honor! Opportunity! Brotherhood!" (p. 76). But these are far from the reality. Mark the following lines :

> ...the greatest nation the world has ever known, where all men are born free and equal, with equal opportunities to all, where the founding fathers have guaranteed to each one happiness, where Truth, Honor, Liberty, Justice and the Brotherhood of Man are a religion absorbed with one's mother's milk, taught at our father's knee, sealed, signed, and stamped upon the glorious constitution of these United States! (p. 76).

Dreams and realities are poles apart. If these are the constitutional mottos of the greatest nation of the world, then where does Yank belong to? Thus, he, throughout the play, is linked with the evolutionary process — a thinking ape. Society, faced with the desire of the beast to become human, places him in cage after cage, condemning him without seeing him, mocking his power and life. And this arouses emotions of protest against a world that victimizes any of its citizens this way. Yank's unconscious self accepts the fact, remembering the world of Mildred, that he is a 'Hairy-ape' in a cage of steel. The word 'hairy-ape' continues to torture him, and he considers prison as a zoo.

In the prison-cell, behind the steel bar, Yank starts realising the naked reality of life. He feels that his power and strength, with which he has been identified throughout, is nothing but a false ego, merely a dream, an illusion. The force which he has thought strength — steel — is in reality no strength at all. The idea that he is steel, he belongs to steel as steel belongs to the industrial world, is completely wrong. He becomes aware that the power, which he has considered his own, does not belong to him; instead, it belongs to Mildred's Father : "Sure-her oldman-President of de Steel Trust — makes half de steel in de world-steel — where I tought I belonged — drivin'trou- movin'in dat — to make her — and cage me in for her to spit on! Christ'" (p. 77).

In modern industralized world there are several Yanks. They have grown up with the faith that they 'belong,' and they think that they are the vital parts of a social order. In fact, they are merely part of a machinery world, which can be replaced according to the need of the machine. Yank's urge for belongingness, his search for identity, carries him to the office of I.W.W., an organization which fights for the workers. Unfortunately, there also he fails to find any answer to his problem. Being suspected by the Secretary of I.W.W. as a spy, he is thrown out of the office. His rejection by the I.W.W. is a terrible shock to his belief. The comment of the Secretary — "Oh, hell, what's the use of talking? You're a brainless ape" (p. 83) — makes him realise that the main source of trouble is not in the society, nor in Mildred, but in himself. He pathetically says :

> So dem boids don't tink I belong... Steel was me, and I owned de woild. Now I ain't steel, and de woild owns me. Aw, hell! I can't see— it's all dark, get me? It's all wrong! (p. 83).

Now, he realises the truth, and becomes aware that the entire system is wrong and there is no real solution to his problem. He thinks as if he were in a state of complete darkness. In fact, O'Neill never suggests any solution to the problems of his characters. He sees no hope for man in his suffering. Whatever hope he sees for man lies in individuals, who may have the courage to possess their own souls. Most individuals, however, he sees hopelessly dehumanized, and his heroes, who are in search of new values, are so ingrown, tormented and doomed that they are not likely to lure one into following their example. Most of O'Neill's really pleasant characters are his conventional, unthinking bourgeois, for at least they are capable of the affection of others. He accepts no answer to life but death. That is what happens in the case of Yank. O'Neill describes the helpless condition of Yank in a more realistic way after he is thrown out of the I.W.W. building. Yank's helpless answer to the policeman shows that he has lost all his way for the sake of his identity. In reply to policeman's question, he says :

POLICEMAN : What you been doin'?

YANK : Enuf to gimme life for! I was born, see? Sure, dat's de charge (p. 84).

When a man loses his way and finds no solution to his problem, he considers his life a curse. Finally, he descends in that position where he thinks that the greatest mistake is nothing but his existence : "In the Stokehole, Yank belongs. His Credo — that he is the force at the bottom that makes the entire mechanized society move — is right. He is such a force until the meeting with Mildred causes him to doubt himself and sends him out in a frenzied effort to destroy the God of power he has served at his furnace alter."[15] But he finds no solution to his problem either in his acceptance or in his rejection.

It is the most difficult task for a man to live alone because he is gregarious by nature. But now Yank is rejected by the society; he does not belong to the human-world. Suffering from this sort of isolation, he tries his best to belong to somewhere, even to the animal-world. Search for identity becomes an obsession with him, and it leads him to the zoo where he stands face to face with a gorilla in its cage and seeks its companionship :

> Ain't we both members of de
> same club—de Hairy Apes? (p. 85).

He considers even the position of Gorilla better than his : "You belong! Sure! Yuh're de on'y one in de woild dat does, yuh lucky stiff!" (p. 85).

Like other human beings, he has neither the sweet past nor the memory of home life by recollecting which he may satisfy himself or get some security. The life he has chosen places him at the point of no return. Pathetically he says to the ape :

> Youse can sit and dope dream in de past, green woods, de jungle and de rest of it. Den yuh belong and dey don't. Den you kin laugh at 'em, see? Yuh're de champ of the world. But me — I ain't got no past to tink in, nor nothin' dat's comin', on'y what's now — and dat don't belong (p. 86).

But this is not the end of his search for identity. To join the class of ape, he invites the ape, and is finally seized, thrown by the brutish animal. Before meeting his tragic end, he says :

> He got me, aw right. I'm trou. Even him didn't tink I belonged....Christ, where do I get off at? Where do I fit in? (p. 87).

With a doubtful note —"And, perhaps, the Hairy Ape at last belong" (p. 86) : — the dramatist ends the play.

When we examine the last sentence in its depth, the question suddenly arises : where does Yank belong to? Torn between two worlds — the animal and the spiritual — he does not know where he stands. Life to O'Neill consists largely in this very struggle of the self with itself — a concept suggested in *The Hairy Ape*; he affirms that the motion and the spirit that impels all thinking is nothing but the search for identity. In saying so, he has extended the symbolism of Yank's struggle beyond psychology to philosophy and, in a sense, to anthropology. The search for identity is not only a personal problem, but becomes the collective universal problem of mankind. Regarding this vital problem of the modern world, Henrich Straumann says : "There is a search for man's true identity, there is an earnest plea for the recovery of clearly established moral and religious values set against an awareness of evil and guilt, and there is a revolutionary will to create new form of expression..."[16]

Yank cannot go forward to the spiritual nor can he go back to nature whence he has came, and so he stands in between, taking all punishment. Finally, he remains an isolated and lonely person. With a deep sense of responsibility, he searches for an image of himself; but he cannot see beyond his conscious self, and the barrier can be overcome only by death.

4. *ALL GOD'S CHILLUN GOT WINGS* (1923)

All God's Chillun Got Wings is the next important play in which man in relation to his social environment and his failure to adjust within the social sphere have been the dramatist's dominant theme. In his plays, he tries to maintain the individuality of his characters, who are the victims of social forces and who ultimately fail to achieve the desired individuality. In their struggle to establish themselves, his characters become isolated beings. What they desire cannot be granted to them, and what they get cannot be desired by them. Sometimes, his characters are in a state of illusion; they are not able to bridge the gap between reality and dream. They try to proceed in their own way but finally fail in their attempts. As a result, they suffer from a sense of isolation and loneliness. Then, obviously, arises the problem of identity, the problem of belongingness. The play *All God's Chillun Got Wings* deals with the same problem. According to Travis Bogard, the play deals with the tragic story of a married couple who are deeply committed to each other, and yet are divided by a profound sense of isolation and loneliness which is the basic cause of their tragedy.[17]

The play deals with the tragic marriage between Jim Harris, the intelligent, sensitive negro boy, and Ella Downey, his white wife. Both are unable to adjust themselves with their circumstances. Growing up in the slum area of New York, in the innocence of childhood, they pledge their love. Jim adores Ella who spurns him when she begins to feel the force of race-prejudice. She lives with Mickey, a white vagabond, and becomes the mother of an illegitimate child. Mickey deserts her and the child dies. In despair, Ella accepts the proposal of marriage of her true worshipper Jim, and they live in France. After two years, they return to New York with the hope that Jim would appear in the Bar examination. But his effort to study law is defeated by his sense of racial pride. Ella is inferior in mind and feeling to her husband, and, in conflict with his mother and sister, is unable to conceal her dislike for his race. She is driven gradually insane by the rejection of both the races. She belongs neither to her own race nor to the race of her husband. By marrying a white girl, Jim also faces the same problem. In the end, vaguelessly both try in vain to return to their childhood so that they may free themselves from the clutches of racial bondage, and finally remain alone.

The play opens in a street, the lower part of the New York City, where Jim and Ella are two innocent children, playing with each other, knowing no difference but of the color. For him, she is 'painty-face; and for her he is 'Whitest among White.' From the very beginning Jim has a fascination for the white race and the underlying cause of it may be Ella, who belongs to that race. Jim considers himself inferior to the white boys of the street because they call him "Jim Crow." In order to change his color, he has tried a lot, as he tells Ella :

> You know what, Ella? Since I been tuckin' yo' books to school and back, I been drinkin' lots o' chalk 'n' water tree times a day. Dat Tom, de barber, he tole me dat make me white, if I drink enough....[18]

His fascination for the white compels him to hate the black; he does not like to be called negro, though he belongs to that race. When Ella consoles him by saying "I'd like to be black" and their friends call her crow, Jim suddenly protests :

> They would't never dast call you nigger, you bet'. I'd kill 'em'.... (p. 94).

From the very beginning he reveals an unconscious hatred of the Negro in himself. The cause behind his indifference may be Ella, her lonely companion from the white race, who consoles him : "I wish I was black like you" (p. 94), and also agrees "I'm your girl" (p. 94). This is the greatest achievement for a negro boy that someone who loves him belongs to a superior race than his. This superiority complex grows in his mind, and for the sake of Ella he unconsciously separates himself from his own race.

With the passage of time everything changes accordingly, except his feelings for Ella whom he has promised not to forget. But with maturity comes the awareness of disharmony between the races. Ella, who once was so much involved with Jim, now begins to hate him for his race. Still Jim keeps her memory in the softest corner of his heart. He can tolerate everything against himself, but not a single word about his sweet heart. When Mickey hints his relation with Ella, Jim violently opposes :

> What — I wanted to say! I know-I've heard-all the stories-what you've been doing around the ward-with other girls — it's none of my business, with them-but she — Ella — it's different — she's not that kind (p. 98).

But on the contrary, Ella does not like to talk with Jim :

JIM : Then why haven't you ever hardly spoken to me-for years?

ELLA : (resentfully) What would I speak about? You and me've got nothing in common any more.

JIM : (desperately) May be not any more-but-right on this corner-do you remember once-?

ELLA : I don't remember nothing! (Angrily) say! What's got into you to be butting into my business all of a sudden like this? Because you finally managed to graduate, has it gone to your head?

JIM : No, I — only want to help you, Ella.

ELLA : Of all the nerve You're certainly forgetting your place! Who's asking you for help, I'd like to know? Shut up and stop bothering me!

JIM : (insistently) If you over need a friend-a true friend — (p. 100).

Inspite of her indifferent attitude, he offers her his friendship, which has been rejected by her :

> I've got lots of friends among my own — kind
> I can tell you (*Exasperatedly*) You make me
> sick! Go to the devil! (p.100).

She clearly makes a dividing line between her and Jim, and refuses friendship with him. But still, he has the same faith, the same devotion towards her. He is teased by the whites for his black skin. This keeps him away from the society of the whites and his fascination for the white race also keeps him separate from the blacks. Joe rightly remarks :

> ....What's all dis fakin' an' pretendin' and swellin'
> out grand an' talkin' soft and perlite? What's all
> dis denyin you's a nigger-an' wid de white boys

> listenin' to you say it! Is you aimin' to buy white wid yo' ol' man's dough like Mickey say?... Tell me befo' I wrecks yo' face in! Is you a nigger or isn't you?....(p.101).

Jim's desire 'to buy white' places him in a state where he is not accepted by the white people nor is he adjusted to his own community. To become a lawyer and to get Ella as his own companion keeps him isolated from both the races. His inner consciousness does not forget his own origin, and his desire never allows him to accept the truth.

Being deceived by the white ruffian Mickey, Ella remembers her old worshipper. The same 'nigger' is the only hope for her. Her conversation with Shorty shows to what an extent she changes herself in order to get security :

ELLA : He's been my only friend.

SHORTY : A nigger!

ELLA : The only white man in the world. Kind and white. You're all black-to the heart (p. 105).

By saying so, she keeps her aloof from her own race and is haunted by the same feeling, the loss of belongingness.

In spite of his racial consciousness, Jim desperately tries to fulfil his dream through hard work, but he never forgets his own origin, his complexity that he is inferior to the white boys. Helplessly he describes his condition at the time of examination :

> I can't explain-just-but it hurts like fire. It brands me in my pride. I swear I know more'n any member of my class. I ought to, I study harder. I work like the devil. It's all in my head-all fine and correct to a T. Then when I'm called on-I stand up-all the white faces looking at me-and I can feel their eyes-I hear my own voice sounding funny, trembling-and all of a sudden it's all gone

> in my head-there's is nothing remembered-and I hear myself stuttering-and give up-sit down-they don't laugh, hardly ever. They're kind. They're good people (*In a frenzy*). They're considerate, damn them! But I feel branded! (pp.107-7).

Even if he knows everything, he is unable to answer in the class room. He considers himself a poor naked boy in comparison to his white classmates. He goes on saying :

> And it's the same thing in the written exams. For weeks before I study all night. I can't sleep anyway. I learn it all, I see it, I understand it. Then they give me the paper in the exam room. I look it over, I know each answer-perfectly. I take up my pen. On all sides are white men starting to write. They're so sure-even the ones that I know nothing. But I know it all — but I can't remember any more-it fades-it goes-it's gone. There's a blank in my head-stupidity-I sit like a fool fighting to remember a little bit here, a little bit there — not enough to pass-not enough for anything-when I know it all! (p. 107).

Although Jim has prepared well, but fails to write a bit at the time of examination. The real problem of his failure is nothing but the racial consciousness that is deep-rooted within his mind. He is free outwardly, but psychologically he is in bondage. His only problem is how to belong. He fails to answer because he considers himself a misfit to his circumstances and ultimately becomes an isolated person in the midst of white students. Doris V. Falk rightly remark in this context :

> He has deliberately renounced his hated self in order to attain an impossible self-image. Marrying Ella and becoming a lawyer are for Jim part of the unconscious longing to achieve what he thinks it means to be "white." His drives are what Horney

> calls "tyrannic shoulds," and his fear that he can never fulfill these demands makes him crawl in constant apology to himself and society.[19]

This unconscious desire to be a 'white' has constantly been supported by Ella since his childhood days. Infact, it is nothing but a fantasy, merely an illusion. Still he satisfies his pride by her consolation : "You have been white to me" (p. 107). Being cheated and cut-off from Mickey, Ella becomes insecure and needs someone's help who can give her security and identity. She helplessly expresses :

> I'm alone. I've got to be helped. I've got to help some one — or it's the end-one end or another (108).

But who else can give a security to an ex-prostitute except Jim, who has been waiting for her since his childhood and whose only ambition is to please her. He eagerly says :

> Oh, I'll help — I know I can help — I'll give my life to help you-that's I've been living for — (108).

His vain effort to identify himself with the white race becomes a passion for him. He is ready to go to any extent for her love. Truly, his love for Ella is not merely a relation between a man and a woman; it is a devotion that keeps him away from his own being and makes him forget about this origin. He has conceded to leave everyone, even his own land, for her sake and her satisfaction. Her helplessness and his ambition are united in their marriage. But none of them are free from the racial bondage. They still have the same guilt-complexity within themselves. It seems that the races meet and converge, but do not really mingle.

But all these blue hopes for a new life fade away. Being alienated from their own land and people, they are never mentally satisfied. Constantly they suffer from a sense of isolation and try to separate themselves from the general trend. At first Ella shows this type of abnormality. Jim tells to his sister Hattie : "Ella did't want to see anybody" (p. 116). As a loyal husband and a true worshipper of his love,. Jim considers it as a sign of happy life. He thinks that his wife may not like the interference of anybody in their lives. But, contrary to his expectations, things go wrong. Ella slowly enters into the deep layer of racial bondage. She tries to keep herself aloof from everybody. Jim remembers the change :

> But she never did get to wanting to go out any place again. She got to saying she felt she'd be sure to run into someone she knew — from over here. So I moved us out to the country where no tourist ever comes — but it didn't make any difference to her. She got to avoiding the French folks the same as if they were Americans and I couldn't get it out of her mind (p. 116).

In order to get a security, she marries him but never comes out of the racial complexity. She hides herself and suffers from a sense of isolation which affects her mentally as well as physically. Commenting on the play, O'Neill once explained : "The real tragedy is that the women could not see their 'togetherness' — the oneness of Mankind. She was hammed in by inhabitions. Ella of the play loved her husband, but could not love him as a woman would a man, though she wanted to, because of her background and her inherited racial prejudice...."[20] Consequently, Jim is also affected by the same sort of feeling. It gradually develops in their mind. They slowly separate themselves from the crowded street of life. Jim describes it to Hattie :

> We never quarreled a single bit. We never said a harsh word. We were as close to each other as could be. We were all there was in the world to each other. We were alone together (p. 116).

Jim realises that this sort of lonely feeling originates from their escapism and guilt-complexity To him, such an isolation becomes unbearable. He has to attain his goal to fulfil his aim to become a lawyer, and so they return to America. Jim confesses :

> Yes. We decided the reason we felt sort of ashamed was we'd acted like cowards. We'd run away from the thing-and taken it with us. We decided to come back and face it and live it down in ourselves, and prove to ourselves we were strong in our love — and then, and that way only, by being brave we'd free ourselves, and gain confidence, and be really free inside and able then to go anywhere and live in peace and equality with our selves and the world without any guilty, uncomfortable feeling coming up to rile us (pp. 116-17).

Their homecoming in a hope of finding peace is nothing but an illusion. Everything goes contrary to their expectations. Gradually, the awareness of race comes to them. Apropos of this, Francis Fergusson rightly remarks :

> And then the real drama begins : the struggle in Jim between his love for Ellla and his ambition to succeed in the world; the struggle in Ella between her love for Jim and her hatred of him as the cause of her exile from her own people. The point of conflict in Jim's career; for his self respect he needs to become a lawyer, while Ella, who has never really accepted him as her husband, needs to preserve her spiritual ascendancy by preventing him from passing his examinations. Tied together by their love and by their solitude, they alternately take refuse in each other's arms and fight for mastery or vengeance.[21]

At first she considers her marriage as a personal redemption. But, again, it proves an illusion; each of them has felt the peace to be illusory, based on an evasion both of the social and personal issues between them, much as their childish efforts to change their colors has failed to admit the reality of their circumstances. As their awareness of living in a false world grow, Ella begins to withdraw, isolating herself and Jim.

To save themselves from the hostile eyes of the outer world, they choose Jim's parental house as a secure place where they may lead a happy life. But to their hard luck, there waits a black world consisting of black people and black atmosphere. O'Neill gives a detailed description of the flat where they have to stay :

> .... A flat of the better sort in the Negro district...on one wall, in a heavy gold frame, is a coloured photograph — the portrait of an elderly Negro... In the left corner, where a window lights it effectively, is a Negro primitive mask from the Congo — a grotesque face, inspiring obscure, dim connotations in one's mind, but beautifully done, conceived in a true religious spirit. In this room, however, the mask acquires an arbitrary accentuation.... (p. 112).

The Congo mask, a wedding presentation from Jim's sister Hattie, especially plays a vital role to arouse racial consciousness in the mind of Ella. It seems Hattie tries to make them aware of their origins. The sense of shame of being black, shame born bitterly of his love for Ella, brings him into conflict with the play's principal racial symbol, the Congo mask. Ella's first sight of it causes her to recoil, as she recognizes in it all the elements of black color that terrify her. Although she tries to ignore the hidden truth behind the mask, but it is clear that she considers the mask to be the source of her shame, as it symbolises the black heritage of her husband. She gives a mock-reply to Hattie :

> I'm not scared of it if you're not (Looking at it with disgust) Beautiful? Well, some people

> certainly have queer notions! It looks ugly to me and stupid-like a kid's game-making faces! (She slaps it contemptuously) Pooh! you need n't look hard at me. I'll give you the laugh. (p. 119).

The entire surrounding in which she has to live compels her to consider herself a lonely white prisoner in the world of negroes. The furniture, the portrait of Jim's father and the racial pride of Hattie constantly shock her. She says :

> It's his old Man-all dolled up like a circus horse! Well they can't help it. It's in the blood, I suppose. They're ignorant, that's all there is to it (*she moves to the mask-forcing* a mocking tone) Hello, Sport! who d' you think you're scaring? Not me! I'll give you the laugh. He won't pass, you wait and see. Not in a thousand years! (*she goes to the window and looks down at* the street and mutters) All black! Every one of them!.... (p. 120).

She is so much divided by the racial bondage that it is almost impossible on her part to keep herself away from the superior feelings of the 'white'. Therefore, she suffers from a lack of belongingness. She belongs neither to her own race nor she is able to fit herself in Jim's world. Her vain attempt to deny the power of mask makes a barrier between Jim's ambition and her pride. She fears the mask which represents the blackness in Jim, to which she cannot belong. Being defeated by life and cheated by Mickey, Ella accepts Jim, but she is not able to cross the racial barrier. The marriage to her is, in spite of her gratitude to Jim, a symbol of her final degradation. Gradually, her hatred for her husband grows, and with it her guilt. At all costs she must establish her superiority over him. She does so by destroying his self-confidence so that he is incapable of passing the Bar Examination he has been studying for. She fears that after passing the Bar Examination, he will be above her position, above her own race, and this is unbearable to her. She becomes more and more abnormal day by day, and reaches a position where she calls Jim a 'dirty nigger.'

Undoubtedly, she loves Jim, but she wants to keep him and herself away from his race so that they can enjoy a life of their own. Unfortunately, her hope is shattered by his ambition. She cannot stop identifying Jim with the Congo mask, and suffers from the conflict which reaches the climax in Scene III of Part II, where Ella talks to the Congo mask : "...What're you grinning about, you dirty nigger, you? How dare you grin at me? I guess you forget what you are" (p. 129).

Finally, Jim fails in his Bar Examination, and this is what she wants. She remarks : "Oh, Jim. I knew it! I knew you couldn't'. Oh, I'm glad, Jim! I'm so happy! You're still my old Jim-and I'm so glad" (p.131). In a frenzy, she stabs the mask and says : "it' all right, Jim! It's dead. The devil's dead. See! It couldn't live-unless you passed. If you'd passed it would have lived in you. Then I'd have had to kill you, Jim don't you see? — or it would have killed me. But now I've killed it" (p.131). By stabbing the mask, she finally denies her belongingness to the race of her husband.

Thereafter, Ella's triumphant escape into madness forces Jim to give up his goal and to live with her in the diminishing cell. She now realises that she has ruined him, and Jim has no other alternative but to accept her affirmatively as his destiny. Both of them try to go backward, as they are not able to adjust themselves with the forward movements. At the end of the play, Jim cries :

> Forgive me, God-and make me worthy : How I see your Light again! Now I hear your voice!... Forgive me, God, for blaspheming you! Let this fire of burning suffering purify me of selfishness and make me worthy of the child you send me for the women you take away (p.133).

Ella consoles her : "Don't cry Jim! You must n't cry! I've got only a little time left and I want to play. Don't be old uncle Jim now. Be my little boy, Jim. Pretend you're painty face and I'm Jim Crow. Come and play" (p. 133). In his final words Jim agrees : "I'll play right up to the gates of Heaven with you" (p.133). Far away lies his vision from this world. It is seated in his personal relationships with her. He feels that beyond his desire and struggle, aspiring to be the Child of God, he can conquer fate and achieve happiness.

In his search for human values, O'Neill faces unsurpassable barriers that divide man against man. Through his dramatic skill, he analyses the tragedy of man's state of isolation and feeling of loneliness in various ways. He dramatizes man's quest for understanding, love, affection, and belongingness in the midst of disruptive forces at work against human solidarity. On the surface, the play seems to deal with the problem of miscegenation. But actually it is a tragedy of man's isolation and loneliness. Both Jim and Ella fail to 'belong' to anyone and anywhere. They cannot even belong to each other. Though the title conveys the message of man's professed faith that "All God's Chillun Got Wings," there are several barriers that separate God's one child from another. Jim might have got 'wings'; he has the new hope with him but his hope, entirely based on illusion, remains an illusion.

REFERENCES

[1] Arthur and Barbara Gelb, *O'Neill* (New York : Harper, 1962), p. 334.

[2] Eugene O'Neill, *Beyond the Horizon and Macro Millions* (London : Jonathan Cape, 1960), p. 5. Hereafter, all the quotes from *Beyond the Horizon* will refer to this edition and be indicated only by the page number in parenthesis in the body of this study.

[3] Arthur and Barbara Gelb, *O'Neill*, p. 335.

[4] Doris V. Falk, *Eugene O'Neill and The Tragic Tension* (New Jersey : Rutgers Univ. press, 1958), p. 41.

[5] Quoted by J.W. Krutch in "Introduction" to *O'Neill, Nine Plays* (New York : Modern Library, 1941), p. xvii.

[6] Eugene O'Neill, "What the Theatre Means to Me," *O'Neill and His plays*, ed. Oscar Cargil *et al.* (New York : New York Univ. press, 1961), pp. 110-11.

[7] Julias Bab, "As Europe Sees America's Foremost Playwright," *O'Neill and His plays*, p. 350.

[8] O'Neill, *Nine Plays*, p. 5. Hereafter the quotes from *The Emperor Jones* will refer to this edition and be indicated only by the page number in parenthesis in the body of this study.

[9] Camilo Pellizzi, "Irish-Catholic Anti-Purtian," *O'Neill and His Plays*, p. 354.

[10] Doris V. Falk, *Eugene O'Neill and the Tragic Tension*, p. 67.

[11] *O'Neill and His Plays*, pp. 110-11.

[12] Eugene O'Neill, *Nine Plays* (New York : Modern Library, 1941), p. 43. Hereafter, the quotes from *The Hairy Ape* will refer to this edition and be indicated only by the page number in parenthesis in the body of this study.

[13] Andrew, E. Malone, "Eugene O'Neill's Limitation", *O'Neill and His Plays*, ed. Cargil, p. 261.

[14] Heinrich Straumann, *American Literature in the Twentieth Century* (London : Arrow Books, 1951), p. 19.

[15] Travis Bogard, *Contour in Time : The Plays of O'Neill*, (New York : Oxford Univ. Press, 1972), p. 247.

[16] Henrich Straumann, *American Literature in the Twentieth Century* (London : Arrow Books, 1951), p. 23.

[17] Travis Bogard, *Contour in Time : The Plays of O'Neill* (New York : Oxford Univ. Press, 1972), p. 191.

[18] Eugene O'Neill, *Nine Plays* (New York : Modern Library, 1941), p. 94. Hereafter, the quotes from *All Gods Chillun Got Wings* will refer to this edition and be indicated only by the page number in parenthesis in the body of this study.

[19] Doris, V. Falk, *Eugene O'Neill and the Tragic Tension* (New Jersey : Rutgers Univ. Press, 1958), p. 88.

[20] Arthur and Barbara Gelb, *O'Neill* (New York : Harper and Brothers, 1969), p. 536.

[21] Francis Fergusson, "Melodramatist," *O'Neill and His Plays*, ed. Cargil *et al.*, p. 275.

3

The Middle Phase

This chapter explores the theme of isolation and loneliness in *Desire Under the Elms* (1924), *The Great God Brown* (1925), *Strange Interlude* (1927) and *Mourning Becomes Electra* (1931), The common features of these plays are adultery, insanity and possessiveness. The most important characters, especially the protagonists, are victims of their situations and, for the most part, play in the hands of fate. Owing to their mental conflict and insecurity, they struggle hard to get a place either in society or in the heart of some specific person. But their ill-luck stands like rock in their way, and isolates them from one another. They have lost the harmony of situations. One of the notable features about these plays is that they are dominated by the female characters. The male characters are puppets in the hands of their woman counterparts. These plays are concerned with the story of the family, and are not like the plays of the Early Phase which deal, for the most part, with racialism, nor are they like those of the Later Phase which are based on the autobiographical element. Another common feature of these plays is the concept of God. In *Desire Under the Elms*, we find Ephraim Cabot as the worshipper of hard-god; in *The Great God Brown*, we watch Cybel in the form of mother-earth; and we notice Nina Leed's assumption of mother-god in *Strange Interlude*. One can easily feel the Hellenic influence on O'Neill in these plays. As regards the dramatic techniques, the dramatist has employed Masks, soliloquies and asides frequently to expose the hidden motif of his characters, and thus he makes a landmark in the realm of American theatre.

Man's inner conflict and his suffering in utter loneliness fascinate Eugene O'Neill. He effectively delineates this isolated state of man through his dramatic skill. Sometimes, man's own ego is responsible for his suffering, while at times he is forced by some outer force. Ultimately, through this conflict, he reaches a state of isolation. O'Neill's *Desire Under the Elms* reveals the same story of conflict in the mind of its characters that arises from their desire to possess. It dramatises the fierce struggle of three main characters to possess a rock-bound farm in order to give a direction and meaning to their insecure and lonely lives. Their quest is similar to that of Yank; basically they desire something to which they can 'belong.' In their search for belonging, they pass through one illusion to another and at every step the cold touch of reality disillusions them. In the way of belonging, they lack the real communication and become alien to one another.

1. *DESIRE UNDER THE ELMS* (1924)

Desire Under the Elms (1924) deals with the tragedy of a New England farmer of 1850's, Ephraim Cabot, who is unable to communicate either with his wives or with his sons. His belief of a *hard God* and his fierce possessiveness of a rocky farm prevent him from achieving a harmonious relationship with the members of his family. In order to escape the tyrannic eyes of their father, Simeon and Peter, the first two sons from the first wife, leave the house after selling their shares to Eben, their half-brother. In the meantime. Ephraim marries for the third time, at the age of seventysix, Abbie Putnam, a young and voluptuous widow of thirty-five. His step son Eben is filled with resentement because he will thus be disinherited from the farm which belonged to his deceased mother. As Ephraim is impotent owing to his old age, Abbie starts seducing young Eben in order to have a child by him so that she might claim for Ephraim's farm.

Finally, she becomes the mother of a son, whom Ephraim believes as his own. Having come to know that he is the instrument of his own disinheritance, Eben becomes furious at Abbie. She, while seducing him really falls in love with him; and to prove her fidelity she kills the new born baby. After realising that he is also responsible for the crime committed by her, both he and Abbie surrender themselves to law, leaving the old Cabot sitting lonely in the best farm of the country.

The title of the play symboilzes that the persons who seek shelter under the 'Elms' have several desires within. The setting — the visible exterior and interior — stresses the separateness of the characters in the play. The alternation between interior and exterior signifies both the domestic lives of the characters and of the farm which is the sole aim to their lives and a consuming object of their desires. The father, who worships a *hard God*, always sticks to his possession. The two elder sons roam about the gold-field of California, and the third one desires the possession of the entire farm from his greedy father. Even the new member of the family, Abbie, steps under the 'Elms' with her desire of possession to get a secure place, to get a new identity of her own. They all try their best to fulfil their ambitions in their own way. Thus, before entering the possessive world of desire, O'Neill describes :

> The South end of the house faces front to a stone wall with a wooden gate at center opening on a country road. The house is in good condition but in need of paint. Its walls are a sickly grayish, the green of the shutters faded. Two enormous elms are on each side of the house. They bend their trailing branches down over the roof. They appear to protect and at the same time subdue. There is a sinister maternity in their aspect, a crushing, jealous absorption. They have developed from their intimate contact with the life of man in the house

> an appalling humaneness. They brood oppressively over the house. They are like exhausted women resting their sagging breasts and hands and hair on its roof, and when it rains their tears trickle down monotonously and rot on the shingles.[1]

The setting not only evokes the nature of stony farm, but it also symbolises the dominance of female characters, represented by the Elms trees, in the play. In the light of psychoanalysis, it may be explained as a symbol of the maternal spirit. It interprets Eben's case as a struggle between two masks, the proud paternal and the submissive maternal. The Oedipus Complex fits into the structure of the play because Ephraim Cabot strikes as the Primordial father and the longing of Eben for his mother is silenced only when he has an incestuous love affair with Abbie.

The conflict between human desire and puritanism is also expressed by the setting. The sky above the roof is suffused with deep colours and the green colour of the elms glows; but the house, in shadow, seems pale and washed out by contrast. The green elms glow with natural passion, while the farm-house is infected with Puritanism. The Stone walls symboilze Ephraim's *hard God.*

When the play opens, Ephraim Cabot is absent from the house. His sons are discussing about his hard nature and their longings and desires. It seems they are lonely men, living in an isolated land, walking hopelessly through the tired routine of their lives with the desire only to possess something by which they may satisfy themselves. Simeon and Peter are dreaming about the gold field of California, whereas Eben's dream is to possess the farm. Both the desires are unconsciously associated with women. Simeon's restlessness is merely a reaction to the loss of Jenn, his deceased wife, and Eben's desire of possessing the farm is associated with his dead mother from whom, as he believes, his father has stolen the farm.

Simeon and Peter are disgusted with the life, provided to them by their father. They are aware of the hardships they have met in cultivating the stony land of their father. They are so much disgusted with him that they do not hesitate to wish him dead or mad. It clearly indicated the Ephraim's principle of worshipping the *hard God* is solely responsible for the isolated lives of his sons. No one is free from the tyrannous eyes of Ephraim. Eben accuses his brothers who did not stand beside their mother when she was suffering and leading a lonely life. Eben believes that the spirit of his dead mother still haunts the house.

Eben's desire to possess the farm is a type of unconscious revenge upon his father's tyranny. He accuses Ephraim for the fatal end of his mother :

> She'd got too tired. She'd got too used t' bein' too tired. That was what he done (*with vengeful passion*) An' sooner 'r later, III meddle. I'II say the thin's I did't say then t'him : 'I'II yell 'em at the top o' my lungs. I'II see t' it my man gits some rest an' sleep in her grave (p.183).

All the three brothers are leading isolated lives. The first two are cut-off from all the warm sides of life, and the third one confines himself to the kitchen which is haunted by the spirit of his mother. There is no cordial relationship between Eben and the elder brothers. Their sense of possessiveness keeps them mentally apart from one another when Simeon and Peter are planning for their monetary condition :

EBEN : (decisively). But t' aint that. ye won't never go because ye'll wait here fur yer share o' the farm, thinkin' allus he'll die soon.

SIMEON : (after a pause) : we've a right.

PETER : Two-thirds belongs t' us (p. 142).

When they assert their rights over the property, Eben violently opposes : "Ye've no right. She wa'n't year Maw; it was her farm. Didn't he steal it from her? She's dead. It's my farm" p. 148).

Eben's visit to prostitute Minne signifies much more than the physical attraction of a male to a female. In spite of knowing that his brothers and father have slept with her, he is proud of his relationship with her. In every respect he wants to share with his father's possession. Eben says : "What do I care fur her — 'ceptin' She's round an' wa'm? The p'int she was his'n — an' she b'long t'me :" (p. 148). Even Simeon has the same sort of feeling in this respect. By revealing the secret to Eben about her relationship with their father, he says, "Ay-eh' we air his heirs in everythin!" (p. 144).

Hearing the news of Ephraim's marriage Simeon and Peter decide to leave the house in order to search a new life where they can be free from the hard principles of their father. At the same time, they discuss about the fate of Eben after their departure. On the other hand, Eben sticks to his possession of the farm, and believes that the whole property belongs to him. He gives the reason : "It's Maw's farm agen! It's my farm! Them's my cow! I'll milk my durn fingers off fur cows o' mine!" (p. 151). He is even ready to pay for the share of his brothers. Simeon's and Peter's search of new life compels them to be alienated from their own land, and so they sell their share to Eben for six hundred dollars.

In the meantime, Ephraim returns with his newly married wife, Abbie, whose marriage to Ephraim is entirely based on her self-interest. It is for security that she marries Ephraim. She narrates the insecure life of her by-gone years to Eben thus :

> I've had a hard life, too — oceans o' trouble an' nuthin' but wuk fur reward, I was an orphan early an' had t' wuk fur others in other folks' hums. Then I married an' he turned out a drunken spreer an' so he had to wuk fur others an' me too agen

> in other folks' hums, an' the baby died, an' my husband got sick an' died too, an' I was glad sayin' now I'm free fur once, on'y I diskivered right away all I was free fur was t' wuk agen in other folks' hums' doin' others folks' wuk till I'd most give up hope O'ever doing my own wuk in my own hum, an' them your paw come... (p.160).

After passing such an insecure phase, naturally aspires a secure life to which she can belong. She keeps her eyes on Ephraim's property which is the real security for her. Abbie's greed and possessiveness for the farm motivate all her actions in the beginning. As soon as she enters the house, she feels that the entire property belongs to her. Her strong determination of possessiveness can be felt from her outward appearance.

It is difficult on her part to suppress the strong urge for desire. Looking towards the house, she exclaims : 'It's purty — purty : I can't blive it's rally mine' (p.155). It seems as if she has got everything which she had desired for a long time. Both Simeon and Peter have left the house, and therefore the only obstacle in her way is young Eben and she thinks she can easily win him. In her encounter with Eben, she tries to win his sympathy by telling him her story of loneliness and hardship. But it seems too difficult on her part to mould him for her purpose owing to his strict sense of possessiveness. After listening to the story, he says to her : 'An! bought yew — like a harlot.... An' the price he's payin' ye — this farm — was, my Maw's, damn ye! — an' mine now!" (p. 160). Abbie is so determined in her mission that the words of Eben hardly matter to her. She replies : "(*defying him*) This be my farm-this be my hum — this be my kitchen!" (p. 161). Her immediate response to the farm reveals her greed and possessiveness. From the very beginning, she smells the mutual physical attraction between Eben and herself, and is confident of winning him. On the other hand, Eben is confused although he appears to be determined to fight her out.

The foremost reason behind Abbie's desire of possession is her sense of insecurity. She has suffered a lot in her past, and hence the real cause of her possessiveness is her desire for security. She wants to belong. She wants to identify herself with the farm of Cabot. This sense of belongingness leads her to establish an illegal relationship with Eben. What she needs is an heir of her own through whom she can assert her authority over the farm, and for that she decides to use Eben as an instrument.

Gradually, Eben is trapped by her sensuality. His longing for the lost mother's urge finds a ray of hope in Abbie. His search for a lost maternity compels him to be a victim of Abbie's lust and purpose. Eben's "quest for the source of feminine power in the land sets him apart from his brothers and brings him into fatal opposition with Ephraim and his *hard God*."[2] Like Simeon and Peter, at first, he seeks satisfaction in a dream of meterial possession; but as the play proceeds, it becomes clear that his hatred for his father and his legalistic claims of ownership are only signals of a truer desire to rediscover the security through an identification with the land. For Eben, the true, the consummate condition of 'being' is to belong to the land as an unborn child belongs to the womb.

In reality, Eben is opposite of his father and his brothers. He has an undefined poetic sensitivity and gift of feminity about him. He is the hero touched with poetry. But unlike Robert Mayo, he is not sentimental, talking out his frustration in a longing for beauty. He has in him a repressed vitality, an animal quality, that gives him maturity and manliness foreign to the earlier dreamer. Yet, like Mayo, he reveals the same need to belong. He seeks the same identification with nature and moves listlessly in alien places like the kitchen — the world of women where he can seek no roots.

Abbie successfully tries to hit the nail of 'purpose' in the soft layer of Eben's sentiment and successfully exploits him in the name of his mother for her own purpose. With their physical union in the room of Eben's mother, the haunted spirit of his mother returns to her grave. The room loses its oppressiveness, tomb-like atmosphere. Both Abbie and Eben discuss it as follows :

ABBIE : ... This room's been dead long enuf. Now it's goin' t' be my room!'

EBEN : (frowning) Ay-eh

ABBIE : (hastly) I meant — our room

EBEN : Ay-eh

ABBIE : We made it our'n last night, didn't we? We give it life-our lovin' did.

EBEN : (with a strange look) Maw's gone back t' her grave. She kin sleep now (p.130).

This shows how successfully Eben is trapped by the scheme of Abbie. She not only proceeds in her 'purpose' of getting an heir for her own security, but also asserts her possession of the room of Eben's mother. Eben becomes conscious of the motive behind her love when a son is born to her. Being aware of her real intention, he threatens to leave her. On the other hand, during the process of seduction, she desperately falls in love with him. In fact, she is so deeply attached to him that she cannot convince him that in the beginning she did make love to him for an ulterior purpose. She frantically tells him that she loves him for his own sake; but he does not listen to her. Therefore, in order to prove that her love for him is neither for the child nor for his inheritance, she kills the child.

After the murder of the child, Eben becomes aware of his guilt. He realises that he is also responsible for the infanticide committed by Abbie. He thinks that he has forced her for the sin. His conscience pricks him and compels him to share with her punishment. As a result, both of them surrender before law. Their war for material possession ends with the crime. They get neither the property nor any security of their own.

They may be satisfied with their love, but one cannot deny the fact that the gap between the old Cabot and the lovers remains unbridged throughout. They are alienated socially with their imprisonment, and thus will be expiated in a long and solitary process.

Though the play seems to deal with the story of two young lovers, yet actually the real spirit behind the play is Ephraim Cabot who dominates the action from the beginning to the end by his indomitable will-power and stone-like strength. Throughout his life he works hard, but suffers in loneliness in search of human understanding. He fails to establish any harmonious relationship with others except the rocks and stones of his farm. No one but he himself is responsible for the barrier created by him on account of his possessiveness, ownership and his belief in *hard God.* There is hardly any cordial relationship between the father and the sons. They have suffered a lot by obeying and following the hard principles of their father :

EBEN : Didn't he slave Maw t' death?

PETER : He's slaved himself t' death. He's slaved Sim 'n' me 'n' yew t' death — on'y none hain't o'us died — yit (p. 141).

On the other hand, Ephraim is also haunted by a sense of loneliness and insecurity. He is worried, thinking about the future of his hard earned farm. This sense of loneliness increases when Simeon and Peter leave the farm. Helplessly, he is in search of a right heir for his possessions which cause a sense of insecurity within him. But to his ill-luck Eben is "Soft-headed Like his Maw Dead Spit 'n' image. No hope in him'... A born fool!" (p. 182).

Ephraim's possessiveness, his belief in *hard God* and his sense of superiority make a wall within himself and the others. What he considers a good life is nothing but the life of hardship, self-denial, and struggle for which he hates those who seek an easy life. His talking of *hard God* and *easy God* distinguishes him as well as his life from the rest. His belief in *hard God* and his total identification with this force is the direct cause of his alienation.

Ephraim wonders whether any man or woman really understands him. His devotion to *hard God* prevents him from establishing any relationship with others. Desperately he tells the tragedy of his isolated life to Abbie, and says how he has been misunderstood by his sons.

> All the time I kept gittin' lonesomer. I tuk a wife. She bores Simeon an' Peter. She was a good woman... She wuked hard... She never knowed me. She helped but she never knowed what she was helpin'. I was allus lonesome (pp. 172-73).

When Ephraim finishes, he finds a blankness on Abbie's face and realizes that he has been wasting his time, narrating what she can never understand. In fact, during his narration, her heart was with Eben.

He also fails to make any understanding even with Abbie. Owing to this lack of communication and his belief in *hard God*, he remains as a lonely man throughout his life. The voice on the wilderness has led him to Abbie, but in her presence as in the presence of other women, he feels alienated from his God, and more lonesome than before. It is as if he had been driven by an alien force that stimulates desire and breeds weariness within him. Consequently, he always finds himself in a lonely state. Neither the *hard God* nor any of the women that come in his life are able to fill the solitude of his life. The *hard God* he has served is no longer there to hear him, and as always when women come to the farm, he is wretched in his loneliness. The root cause of his tragedy is that he is never understood by anybody. Having failed to make any understanding with other human beings, he feels cold and uneasy in his house and tries to find peace in his rocky farm.

Ephraim's own complexity keeps him apart even in the

crowded atmosphere of his house. When everyone is celebrating the function of the new born baby, he does not find any peace in his house : "They's no peace in houses, they's no rest livin' with folks. Somethin's always livin' with ye... I'll go t' the barn an' rest a spell...' (p.189).

When he learns about the relationship between Eben and Abbie and the truth about the child, he becomes more helpless. In a fit of madness, he threatnes to burn the farm and says that it is a signal from God for him to seek an easy life in California. But he is aware of the hardship ahead. He knows he has to face a more solitary life then ever before after the imprisonment of Eben and Abbie. He is destined to spend the rest of his life within the stone-walls of his farm.

The desire to possess grows out of the feeling of insecurity, helplessness or instability. Therefore, O'Neill's vision of life is without foundation, without beliefs or creeds, struggling for a symbol of security in a stony land of a new England Farmstead, where Abbie, the young wife, desires a home for security, Simeon and Peter desire freedom from the hard labour of a rock-bound Farm, Eben desires to possess the farm of his mother, and old Ephraim, disappointed by his wives and sons, desires to escape from his tragic sense of aloneness by possessing the farm he has made out of rocky land. Thus, there ensues a war of possession in which all the members of the family are defeated by the sense of isolation.

2. *THE GREAT GOD BROWN* (1925)

The Great God Brown (1925) stands as a mile-stone in the career of Eugene O'Neill because of its technique that suits its theme. Providing mask, the dramatist exposes the hidden motives of the characters and their dual nature owing to which they are separated from one another. The play shows how man's persistent efforts to belong to Nature are thwarted by materialism, Christian asceticism, and socially caused conflicts in the psyche. The play achieved a tremedous popularity in the twenties. In the words of O'Neill himself :

"*The Great God Brown* was the greatest miracle the New York theatre has ever achieved."[3]

The use of mask in this play is an integral part of the theme. The play shows how a man loses identity wearing a mask of unreality, and moves away from his own self. This agony becomes more intensified when he experiences only the torture of the aspired self without sharing any of its creative urges. This reduces him to a mere lifeless mask, instead of being a living creative creature. Besides showing the two faces of man, the mask expresses the basic polaritics inherent in human existence, such as life and death, saint and satan, art and materialsim, and creation and destruction. The growing materialism in the modern world and the lack of communication with others, force a man to wear a mask in order to get security. In a world where illusions appear to be realities, masks are worshipped as real faces, while the real faces cry for recognition.

The Great God Brown deals with the four helpless persons' futile search for happiness. They are : Dion Anthony, the torn and tortured artist; his wife Margaret, his friend William (Billy) Brown; and Cybel the prostitute. They represent conflicting selves as well as conflicting elements in the society. The play begins with a prologue in which we find Dion and Billy, as boys are in love with Margaret. Their fathers are partners in a construction firm. Billy is a simple boy who wears no mask, and obediently promises his parents to study architecture. But Dion wears a mask of Pan to conceal his real poetic nature. He is too sensitive to stand in the misunderstanding of the world. Margaret loves Dion's mask, which protects his sensitive nature from intrusion, and never comes to know his inner self. She, without ever understanding him, marries him and bears him children. It is here that the play properly opens in their ugly home. The domestic life of the alien couple turns to be a miserable one. Dion has spent his money, and the tenderly loving Margaret suggests him to work for his friend, Billy, now the successful businessman

William A. Brown. Dion hesitatingly sends her to get the job for him. After knowing the reality through Margaret about Dion's failure as an artist and a father, Brown agrees to take him as the chief draftsman in his firm. Instead of painting the nature, Dion becomes a building designer.

Being dissatisfied with life, Dion seeks consolation from Cybel who embodies the honest qualities of earthly love. She accepts him without his mask. But here Dion also finds Brown to be his competitor as he was in the case of Margaret. Brown is jealous of Dion's creativity, though the latter has played a significant role to promote his business. After long and bitter circumstances, Dion mockingly wills Brown his mask, and the latter puts it on and tries to fulfil his desire of possessing Margaret in the disguise of Dion. Replacing his own identity with Dion's mask, he manages for a time to alternate between the two selves, but is unable to continue to play the double role : one as Dion, and the other as Brown. He then assumes the character of Dion for good, and is accused of murdering Brown. In a confused chase by the police who accuse him of murder, Brown is shot. He dies in the arms of Cybel, who affirms the existence of God and love. Disillusioned Margaret finds fulfilment in a state of falsity with her sons and her timeless love for the mask of Dion.

Wearing a mask is not a matter of choice. Man is trapped in the mask by circumstances, and by his own fears and inhibitions. When he fails to find some communion with the world beyond his cells, he separates himself from all other human beings. But his solitary journey never ends until his doom. This happens in the life of Dion Anthony, the distinguished character of the play. When we first meet him, he appears a stranger even in the company of his parents. O'Neill describes him in the following manner :

> ...lean and wiry, without repose, continually in restless nervous movement. His face is masked.

> The mask is a fixed forcing of his own face-dark spiritual poetic, passionately super-sensitive, helplessly unprotected in its child like, religious faith in life-into the expression of a mocking, reckless, defiant, gayly scoffing and sensual young Pan.[4]

The lack of communion with others in the main cause of Dion's alienation. Nobody understood him properly, not even his childhood friend, Billy, whose hostility has compelled him to use the mask for the first time to hide his real self. Ironically, he discloses the fatal incident that has changed his entire life :

> Listen! one day when I was four years old, a boy sneaked up behind when I was drawing a picture in the sand he couldn't draw and hit me on the head with a stick and kicked out my picture and laughed when I cried. It wasn't what he'd done that made me cry, but him! I had loved and trusted him and suddenly the good God was disproved in his person and the evil and injustice of Man was born! Every one called me cry-baby, so I became silent for life and designed a mask of the Bad Boy Pan in which to live and rebel against that other boy's God and protect myself from his cruelty (p. 64).

Thus, the innocent boy, at the age of four, experienced the sudden shocking awareness that God was to the neither loved nor trusted. Humble, meek and pure at heart, the little boy discovered not the kingdom of heaven, but a world of evil and injustice. This proved to be a death-blow to his concept of friendship and artistic aspiration. In order to protect himself from further assault, he caged himself in the mask of bad boy, Pan. But this was the begining of his suffering. The materialistic attitude of his father added fuel in his agony. For his father, money was the only means of living, and so he did not want him to continue his study because "colleges turn out lazy loafters to sponge on their poor old father! Let his slave like I had to! That will teach him the value of a dollar!" (p.12). In this context, we are reminded of the attitude of Ephraim Cabot and his worship of hard-god. Like the old Cabot of *Desire Under the Elms*, he imagines as if he were the God, the father, who has every right to design the future of his son. This is the foremost reason owing to which Dion is separated from his father since his childhood. Dion's wish to paint a beautiful painting is marred by his father's dictatorship. His father tells him : "you'll learn to be a better architect...or I'll turn you out in gutter without a penny" (p.13). In place of a loving father, he finds a cold-hearted businessman and remains a stranger to him. Inevitably he awfully recollects his lonely childhood :

> What aliens we were to each other! When he lay dead, his face looked so familiar that I wondered where I had met that man before. Only at the second of my conception. After that we grew hostile with concealed shame (p. 45).

The painful revelation of the early childhood possesses him entirely, and he can not rest until the promise is somehow fulfilled. So, cut-off from his friend and father, he desperately wants to communicate his real self to his beloved, but finds her only in love with his masked self. When he tries to show his inner self, she recoils with horror. He realizes that there is no human being whom he can comprehend or whose comprehension enables him to unmask himself, and thus free himself from loneliness.

After his marriage and the death of his parents, he becomes more helpless and insecure. Gradually, he loses his interest in life and his family. "His real face has aged greatly, grown more stained and tortured" (p. 25), and his mask becomes "more defiant and mocking, its sneer more forced and bitter, its Pan quality becoming Mephistophelean" (p. 25). He turns to be a split person, tortured by the conflict between his inner-self and the mask. In search of happiness, he becomes spend-thrift drunkard and visits low women. His relation with prostitute Cybel is the result of his longing for his mother's love. Perhaps her mother is the only person who understood his artistic sensibility, and no wonder his father considers him identical to his mother. For him, his mother is the symbol of all the warmth of life that he has lost for ever. He recollets pathetically :

> And my mother? I remember a sweet strange girl, with affectionate, bewildered eyes as if God had locked her in a dark closet without any explanation. I was the sole doll our ogre, her husband, allowed her and she played mother and child with me for many years in that house until at last through two tears I watched her die with the shy pride of one who has lengthened her dress and put up her hair. And I felt like a forsaken toy and cried to be buried with her, because her hands alone had caressed without clawing. She lived long and aged greatly in the two days before they closed her coffin (p. 45).

In search of understanding and love, he marries Margaret. But to his ill-luck, instead of loving him, she loves his mask. He expresses the agony of his tragic alienation when he says to his wife mockingly : "This domestic diplomacy! We communicate in code — when neither has the other's key!" (p. 28). He becomes a stranger to his wife and loses the feelings of a devoted husband. Pretending his failure as an artist when Margaret approaches Brown for a jub to him, he considers it her pride, and not her loyalty. Similarly, when Cybel reminds him about his worried wife, he says :

> She knows-but-she'll never admit to herself that her husband ever entered your door. (Mocking) Aren't women loyal-to their vanity and their other things! (pp. 51-52).

Since in his view "girls only allow themselves to look at what is seen" (p. 20), he considers himself a money-making machine for his family. Living a life of stranger he realizes the hypocrisy. Actually, Dion is disgusted with his playing the role against his will. He is not satisfied with the life provided to him. Instead of painting waves on the sea and the skimming flight of clouds over the tops of tress, he is forced to sketch the plan for municipal buildings. The dream of a painter is washed away by the growing materialism of the world.

Brown's vindictive attitude and possessiveness are the other factors behind Dion's tragic life. He always finds Brown as a competitor in various ways. Describing the latter's jealously in the case of Cybel, Dion says :

> What first aroused his passion of possess you exclusively, do you think? Because he knew you loved me and he felt himself cheated. He wanted what he thought was my love of the flesh! He feels I have no right to love. He'd like to steal it as he steals my ideas-complacently-righteously (p. 52).

Under the stress of the conflicts between the outer mask and inner self, Dion shatters mentally. His mask acquires a sinister reality and completely overshadows his inner being. He realizes that it is realy difficult to live in a world of strangers under the falsity of the mask. His lonely suffering ends in his death. Before the end he decides to bequeath the mask to william Brown.

The theme of alienation is also projected through the character of William Brown in the play. O'Neill describes him in these words :

> "Brown" is the visionless demigod of our new materialistic myth — a success building his life of exterior things, inwardly empty and resourceless, and uncreative creature of superficial preordained

> social groves, a by-product forces aside into slack waters by the deep main current of life-desire.[5]

He represents the materialistic modern man for whom human relationships have no meaning. He symbolises the anguish of the uncreative man, the despair of the person who cannot dream. In this regard, he reminds us of Andrew Mayo of *Beyond the Horizon*. Like him, Brown is an 'anti-poet' by nature. He says : "I never could memorize poetry with a darn" (p.15). Due to lack of this artistic sensibility he is rejected by Margaret and cheated by Cybel. His possessiveness and envious nature separate him from Dion and force him to wear the mask of Pan to 'possess : He madly accepts the mask of Dion Margaret as his wife and Cybel as his mistress. This is quite ironical that the person, who has forced Dion to wear the mask of falsity, himself seeks shelter under the same mask. O'Neill explains this turn in the play :

> Brown has always envied the creative life-force in Dion-what he himself lacks. When he steals Dion's mask of Mephistopheles he thinks he is gaining the power to life creatively, whereas in reality he is stealing that creative power made self-destructive by complete frustration.[6]

The real tragedy with him is that he cannot create as he is the man without vision, without any artistic capability.

He may be a successful businessman but cannot be a creator. As Dion says, "He couldn't design a Cathedral without it looking like the first supernatural Bank! He only believes in the immortality of the moral belly!" (p. 68). Putting on the mask of Dion, he losses his own identity, is separated from his own self, and turns to be a split person. He tries to merge his identity with the identity of Dion, and plans to live in his disguise to enjoy the fame and fortune of the latter. At the same time, he helplessly asks the mask of Dion in a doubtful tone, "What's that? She'll never believe? She'll never see? She'll never understand? You lie, Devil!" (p. 84). Gradually, he reaches a state of hypocrisy. Kissing the mask, he reveals the reason for loving it. "I love you because she loves you! My kisses of your lips are for her" (p. 85). But it is not the reality. It is merely a dream never to be fulfilled. Rather, it is the self-satisfaction of a hypocrite, separated from his own self and possessing other's fortune. He is compelled to play the role of both Dion and Billy simultaneously, and becomes a split personality.

Brown's hope of possessing Margaret shatters because she never accepts him in his real self. He, in the disguise of Dion, cannot oppose Margaret when she, taking him to be Dion, scolds him. Pathetically, he exclaims : "Poor Billy! Poor Billy the Goat! (*With mocking frenzy*) I'll kill him for you! I'll serve you his heart for breakfast!" (p. 90). Even knowing Margaret's attitude of negligence towards him, he hypocritically cooperates her :

> I tell you I'll murder this God-damned disgusting Great God Brown who stands like a fatted calf in the way of our health and wealth and happiness! (p. 90).

His hope of possessing Margaret is diminished completely when she reveals : "I've never thought of Billy Brown except as a friend, and lately not even that! He's just a stupid old fool" (p. 91).

His desire to get the place of Dion proves futile. He realizes that it is Dion who is enjoying all the fortunes that the desired for a long time. But his tragedy is that he cannot destroy the image of Dion, who is residing with him safely. Brown, the visionless 'demi-god' who has never believed in the supreme power, is now compelled to beg Him for the strength to get rid of the clutches of Dion's mask.

Having changed his identity for the sake of materialistic fulfilment, he is isolated from God. But now he realises his mistake and begs pathetically :

> Mercy, compassionate Saviour of Man! Out of my depth I cry to you! Mercy on thy poor Clod, thy cold of unhallowed earth, thy clay, the Great God Brown! Mercy, saviour! (p.103).

However, it is a partial vision — the half-successful attempt of the acceptance of his power and strength. For, when he touches the mask of Dion he realizes the mistake of denying his own self. The illusion becomes clear. Brown cannot create because creation depends on vision, and Brown, devoid of vision, moves in the dark. What he cannot possess, he destroys, as in childhood he destroyed Dion's sand castle and as he finally destroys himself. In a tone of mocking despair, considering himself the Almighty, he says :

> "Bah"! I am sorry, little children, but your kindgom is empty. God has become disgusted and moved away to some far ecstatic star where life is a dancing flame! We must die without him (*Then addressing the mask harshly*) Together-my friend! You too! Let Margaret suffer! Let the whole world suffer as I'm suffering (p. 103).

With the rejection of supreme power, his tragic suffering of alienated life meets its doom. His death under the mask of Dion also keeps him apart from the real death in the eyes of others. The suffering of Dion and Brown reminds us of the tragedy of Robert and Andrew of the play, *Beyond the Horizon*. Like Mayo brothers, Dion and Brown are opposite to each other by nature. Moreover, like them, both the artist and businessman suffer from alienation by choosing the wrong profession.

Margaret and Cybel, the female counterparts of Brown and Dion, also suffer from a sense of isolation and loneliness like the visionless Brown. Margaret is a practical lady. She can compromise with life easily. In the beginning of the play, she admires the artistic quality of Don, and accepts him as her husband. But when she faces the problem of bread and butter, she forces him to take the job of a designer. Although her practical and compromising nature keeps her away from suffering, but her satisfaction is entirely built on falsity and illusion. She does not care for reality. Earlier, she rejects the inner self of Dion, and later, she accepts the falsity of Brown. In the real sense, she is separated from Dion because she is not satisfied with the life she has spent with him. She reveals this truth of Brown when he is in the disguise of Dion. She discloses her lonely suffering of early life and her indifferent attitude towards Dion :

> ... I could never help you — and all the time. I knew you were so lonely! I could always hear you calling to me that you were lost, but I couldn't find the path to you because I was lost, too! That's an awful way for a wife to feel! (p.87).

After the death of Billy in the mask of Dion, she is left alone with the memory of the latter's love.

On the other hand, Cybel symbolizes the rootlessness of the modern world and its corrupt value-system. Choosing the life of a prostitute, she has separated herself from the society. Since she has not been able to belong to the general trend of the society, she prefers to lead a soiltary life. She finds : "Life's all right, if you let it alone" (p. 42). Her conception of love is entirely different from that of others. She says to Dion : "What makes you pretend you think love is so important, anyway? It's just one of a lot of things you do to keep life living" (p. 49). Being disgusted with life, she says : "What's the good of bearing children? What's the use of giving birth to death?" (p. 53).

But her acceptance of Dion's inner self and her sexless involvement with him reveal a different aspect of her character. She represents both the glory and ignominy of womanhood, highlighting the existence of a vicious circle of corrupt values established by the seekers of her flesh and playing the role of mother for the inumerable, lonely souls in quest of faith in life and love. O'Neill describes her as follows :

> "Cybel" is an incarnation of cyble, the Earth Mother, doomed to segregation as a pariah in a world of unnatural laws but partonized by her segregators who are thus themselves the first victims of their law.[7]

The prevalence of perverted human values in the society makes Cybel war the mask of a prostitute, though she is truly and essentially the incarnation of the warm Earth-Mother. But on the contrary, Margaret does not to wear any mask. Both build their lives on externals. Alienated from the terrifying realities of existence, both of them continue to live in a state of falsity. More or less, all the characters of the play suffer from the sense of isolation and loneliness in different ways. Apropos to this, Travis Bogard rightly remarks :

> Significantly, neither Dion nor Brown finds any genuine Human relationship to sustain him. Both men in the Play love Margaret, but the love is little more than a subject for declamation. Margaret, consumed with her sons and her house work and her unperceiving love for husband, is perhaps intended as an example of one who lets life alone.... With Cybel, Dion has a communion, but again it is not such a profound human relationship that it can redeem life's pain.[8]

3. *STRANGE INTERLUDE* (1927)

Strange Interlude (1927) is the longest play ever written by O'Neill. It is a powerful presentation of man's search for identity, belief and belonging. About its source, the playwright writes :

> ... the story of girl whose aviator fiancee was shot down just before the Armistice.... The girl had gone to pieces from the shock. She had married

> not because she loved the man, but because she wanted to have a child. She hoped through motherhood to win back a measure of contentment from life.[9]

In this play, O'Neill touches many themes, including his favourite one — viz., man's loss of belonging and his dissatisfaction with what he has. Again, it depicts the story of both the outward and inward conflicts.

The play focusses of Nina Leeds, a young lady of twenty-two, who lives with her father, Prof. Leeds. Nina inherits the passionate, selfish hunger for love from her father who determines her fate. Professor Leeds has persuaded her lover, Gordon Shaw, not to marry Nina until he returns from the war. But Gordon is killed in the World War I, and Nina is left with agonizing regret and a sense of guilt. She insists neither upon marriage, nor she surrenders herself physically in the arms of her sweet-heart before he left. After the death of her lover, she hates her father and grows neurotic. Chosen to be a nurse in a soldiers' hospital, she offers herself to wounded warveterans in the name of sacrifice of her dead lover. But the promiscuity, which she thinks of as 'sacrifice', turns out to be a sordid, masochistic attempt at oblivion and brings only further guilt and self-hatred. She is intensely admired by the ineffectual novelist Charles Marsden and the brilliant young physician, Dr. Ned Darrell. But neither of them is willing to marry her. Therefore, after her father's search for the thread that will bid her to life, she marries Sam Evans, a dull Simpleton.

The tragic reversal occurs when Nina learns from her mother-in-law that, unknown to Sam, his family has a long history of hereditary insanity, and that is why, Nina should not bear his child. She deliberately aborts the child. But, for Sam's sake as well as for her own security, She decides to have a baby from some man other the her husband. She successfully persuades Dr. Darrell for this. But before their son is born, Darrell and Nina have fallen in love. Her possessive nature wants her lover and child all to herself. She plans to desert Sam, but Darrell refuses to be party to that crime and leaves on a long journey for years. The son, Gordon, is born and she turns to him to fill her need for love. But, to her ill-luck, the child is more attached to Sam Evans. Sam, believing the child to be his, is inspired by his supposed fatherhood to have confidence in his business career. Thus she loses both Darrell and her son. Sam dies, the affair with Darrell is over and Gordon, her son, flies away after marrying Madeline. Now, she is too old and tired to batter any longer at the wall of self in order to find love from some other person. Finally, she desperately surrenders herself to her silent lover, Marsden, thinking to be the last chance for her feelings of 'belongingness.'

There are many sources of tragedy in O'Neill's plays. The most important of these is man's failure to 'belong' or to finds roots anywhere in this hostile world. The present play depicts the same story of man's anguish, and how he is isolated from himself and from others. The play begins with the study of Prof. Leeds in the small University town of New England. The atmosphere of the room symbolises the deserted character of the old professor who has been isolated from the mainstream of life. He confines himself to the cosy atmosphere of the study : "a fugitive from reality can view the present safely from a distance...."[10] His love for old classics reveals the possessive side of his character. Living in the shadow of these illusory ideals, he keeps himself and his daughter cut-off from the world of reality. He thinks that by keeping Nina away from the reality he would be able to keep her love for himself.

This sense of possessiveness led him to prevent his daughter's marriage because he wanted to keep her with him like an old collection for his study. His sense of fear and egoism that arises from insecurity, stood like a barrier between her and him. From the beginning of his life, Professor Leeds has spent a different life, completely severed from the general, social trend. After the death of his wife, he becomes more insecure. He tells Marsden : "...but it's terrible to be so alone in this...if Nina's mother had lived...my wife...dead!" (p. 290). Therefore, in order to mitigate the pain of solitude, he tries his best to reserve the love of Nina for himself. But the love of Gordon makes a wall of hatred between them. Prof. Leeds admits to Nina :

> It is also true I was jealous of Gordon. I was alone and I wanted to keep your love...I did my best to prevent your marriage. I was glad when he died...I wanted to live comforted by your love until the end (p. 300).

But his well-constructed plot goes against his expectation. In order to free herself from the mental agony, Nina decides to leave her home to serve as a nurse in a military hospital. Not only the 'possessiveness,' but his strong sense of puritanism is also the cause of Nina's revolt against him. In this context, he can well be compared with the old Cabot of *The Desire Under The Ems*. Like Abbie and Eben, Nina rebels against her repressive puritanic father, who denies her all possible opportunities for the fulfilment of her desires. As a result, the possessive father has to spend the last breath of his life in a state of wilderness. In his sanctuary-like home, he is compelled to think about Nina'a hatred for him. In sheer despair, he is bewildered : "...she still must hate?...oh, God I feel cold...alone! this home is abandoned! The house is empty and full of death!" (pp.301-02). He expects to die someday there, lonely and crying for help. This expectation of the professor becomes true very shortly. He dies a helpless death after spending the remaining days of life in utter loneliness. Neither he keeps Nina as his possession, nor is he able to get security for himself in his self-created no man's land. Throughout his life he remains isolated from others. Undoubtedly, he is one of the key characters of the play and under his shadow the entire play moves.

A strong sense of possessiveness can be felt in the character of Nina Leeds, the heroine of the play. She is the most powerful character around whom all the four male characters act like puppets. O'Neill rightly remarks : "*Strange Interlude* is Nina' play."[11] She is the protagonist of the play who lives in a world of unreality, since she does not find anything real to which she can belong. This sense of conflict arises out of her possessivensess, her desire to keep all man she has wanted for herself. An inescapable past becomes her whole life. When she realizes the illusory nature of her quested values, she feels embittered and then moves in another direction in clutch at a new illusion. But she fails to achieve her goal of possession, and remains an alienated person throughout her life.

The tragic story of her life begins with the death of Gordon Shaw, her fiancee, whom she cannot forget throughout her life. Her longing for him and to be the mother of his baby leave her in a state of isolation. Life becomes meaningless for her : "Gordon is dead! What use is my life to me or anyone?" (p. 298). She accuses her father of preventing their marriage. She wanted to be in the possession of Gorden, "But Gordon never possessed me; I'm still Gordon's silly virgin" (p. 299). She awfully regrets for not giving herself to Gorden so that she could have his baby as possession for her security. But now she considers herself as a barren woman, who stands lonely in the wasteland of life. She miserably confesses : "And now I am lonely and not pregnant with anything at all, but — but loathing!" (p. 229). She considers herself a coward on account of her failure to make love with him. She says : "I must pay for my cowardly treachery to Gordon!" (p. 299). Her payment for her guilt becomes horrible for her. From this point, she is separated from her father and this separation leads her to leave him and the home and accept a promiscuous life.

Nina has lost her mental peace owing to the insecurity which arises after the death of Gordon. Her act of promiscuity does not fill the vacuum created within her. After the death of her father, she says to Marsden : "You know-grief, sorrow, love, father — those sounds our lips make and our hands write" (p. 315). The sense of security that she has lost never returns to her. Her first attempt as a nurse proves to be a futile search, but her search for belonging never ends. To satisfy her longing, she decides to marry Sam Evans on the advice of Darrell and Marsden. Both the well-wishers of Nina believe that marriage is the only solution to her problem. After her marriage to Sam Evans, she somehow tries her best to regain her lost sense of security through her baby, who is still in her womb. She says : "I hope it is a boy...healthy and strong and beautiful...like Gordon!" (p. 325). It suggests that Gordon is not only a man for her, but is the symbol of her security, her identity. However, her aspired security, for which she longs, is shattered to pieces when Sam's mother reveals the family-curse of insanity. The cruel fate strikes another blow when Mrs. Evan forces her for an abortion and suggests her to get a baby by somebody, instead of Sam.

The story of insanity creates a gap between the wife and the husband. She loses her interest in him. She thinks : "I only married him because he needed me — and I needed children!" (p. 334). Both Nina and Sam are separated mentally. This separation and the memory of Gordon increase her agony. She begins to forget her duty as a wife. The reason of her dissatisfaction with Sam after the abortion is nothing but the memory of Gordon. She confesses : "...I loved it; so it seemed at times that Gordon must be its real father, that Gordon must have come to me in a dream while I was lying asleep besides Sam!" (p. 351). But her dream shatters with the operation, and a sense of insecurity again clouds over her. By any means, she needs a baby who can give her mental satisfaction as well as security. To satisfy her urge for the security, she chooses Dr. Darrell for the father of her baby, violating all the code and conducts of a loyal wife. At first Darrell refuses; but owing to his pressing desire for her, he is mesmerized to prescribe himself scientifically for the act. On the other hand, she considers her illicit affair as a sacrifice like her previous attempt as a nurse. She thinks :

> Of picking out a healthy male about whom she cared nothing and having a child by him that Sam would believe was his child, whose life would give him confidence in his own living, who would be for him a living proof that his wife loved him (p. 353).

Though her prophecy about Sam proves fruitful, yet she fails to play her own part. She no longer remains faithful to her husband. Gradually, remembering their sexual act, she is inclined towards Darrell. The never ending process reaches a state where she considers Sam a bogus man and Darrell means everything to her. For the sake of her happiness, she wants to desolate Sam in favour of Darrell. Sexual relation seems to be the principal reason behind her misery which she fails to bridge due to the gap between her and the men whom she meets. When she fails to give herself to her fiance, she has a conflict with her father and becomes an alien daughter. Now, for the sake of Darrell, she wants to throw Sam. But when Darrell rejects her proposal of marriage and decides to leave, she wants to avenge him. Instead of breaking down, she thinks to use Sam as an instrument for her revenge. This selfishness and passion for possession keep her apart from her family members and friends.

Not only her sexual jealously, but also the lack of correlation between her thought and action makes her an indifferent lady. Due to her own mistake, she always finds herself in a state of agony and guilt. The security, which she is craving for, is expressed in her thought, not in her action. She realizes that no single man can provide her a sense of fulfilment. So, she tries to get all the men she knows into her trap, and to some extent, she gets the taste of success. As she says triumphantly :

> My three men I feel their desires converge in me...to form one complete beautiful male desire which I absorb...and am whole...they dissolve in me, their life is my life...I am pregnant with the three....! (p. 395).

But this is not truth. It is an illusion which is marred by her cruel and capricious wilfulness and a power to hurt not only herself but all men whom she knows.

Disillusioned by the men, she places all her hopes in Gorden, thinking him to be the last resort of her belonging. She says :

> These men make me sick...I hate all three of them! They disgust me...the wife and mistress in me has been killed by them! Thank God, I am only a mother now! ...Gordon is my little man, my only man....! (p. 406).

Here also luck plays its role contrary of Nina's expectation because her idea of belonging is entirely based on falsity. Her futile pursuance of an unattainable romantic ideal is destroyed by her son, when the latter flies with his beloved. In a state of fear, doubt and loneliness, she loses her faith in God. She does not find a way out to her self-created problems. She fails in her quest for personal happiness, and broods over old age and death, recalling with sentimental retrospection the irrecoverable afternoons of passion. She is tortured by the confusion of truth and reality. In a voice of sad reconciliation she thinks :

> The only living life is in the past and future...the present is an interlude...Strange Interlude in which we call on past and future to bear witness we are living!.... (p. 420).

Nina has always dreamt of love and happiness. But how does her dream shape into reality? The death of her real lover, her betrayal by her father, her horrible experience as a nurse, her tragic marriage with Sam, her physical and emotional involvement with Darrell, and her failure to keep the love for her son Gordon — all her encounters with reality break her till she becomes the ghost of her former self. Where does she belong? She can neither be a lover, nor a wife or a mother.

In the evening of her life, she is left alone with Marsden. Darrell goes back to his work, Sam dies, and her son flies with Madeline. The tragic pull between her need to give and her need to take is over. She is so drained and exhausted emotionally that she wants a security in which she may find her lost sense of belonging, for which she has been struggling throughout her life. Finally, she decides to marry Charles Marsden, her silent lover, to end her long journey of insecurity. She considers life as "merely strange dark interlude in the electrical display of God the Father!" (p. 449).

Another significant character of the play, who suffers a lot through isolation, is Dr. Edmund Ned Darrell. He seems to be the most wanted person in Nina's list of men. Clifford Leech describes him as "much needed then the others of understanding Nina."[12] Professionally, he is a physician; emotionally, an ardent lover; and from human point of view, a weak person. First, we meet him when Nina returns from the hospital. He is a young man of twenty-seven, whose charming physical appearance attracts the attention of a women easily. He is a rootless person having no familiar attachment like Sam Evans or Charles Marsden. He enters the story as a sympathizer to Nina, but turns to be an isolated one due to his deep attachment with her. His hypocritical attitude is the root of his disillusionment because of which he suffers from a deep sense of anguish throughout his life. He is attracted towards Nina in his first meeting, but instead of marrying her, he proposes her for Sam Evans. He admits the truth to Nina later : "Since I first met you, I've always desired you physically" (p. 367). In the beginning, the proud scientist within himself does not allow him to accept the truth. Therefore, he considers his physical involvement with Nina only a scientific approach for breeding children, and love is only the physical union of two guinea pigs. This illusory concept of love is shattered when he finds himself truly in love with Nina. As love is an overwhelming and mysterious power against which neither science nor human will can prevail, Darrell, separated from Nina, no longer finds any interest in his study and ruins his career. To mitigate the pain of separation, he involves with other women but is never able to get satisfaction.

In the search of happiness, he returns to Nina after spending a long period of frustration and separation. He confesses before Nina :

> I wasn't all noble, I'll confess! I thought of myself and my career! Damn my career! A lot of good that did it! I didn't study! I didn't live! I longed for you — and suffered. I paid in full, believe me, Nina! But I know better now! I've come back. The time for lying is past! You've got to come away with me! (p. 391).

But the destiny has played its part. It has left Darrell in a state where he finds himself alone, and helpless before the force of circumstances. He has lost his beloved and his son. Realizing his situation, he asks Nina : "You think I'll stay — to be your lover — watching Sam with my wife and my child—" (p. 392). But he must accept the truth that he has reached the same state of nothingness from where he had started his futile journey for happiness. Submitting himself to the cruel hands of reality, he choses to remain a father alienated from his son and a lover isolated from his sweet-heart for the remaining years of his life.

Charles Marsden is another victim of the disease of romantic imagination. He is the only male figure who came in contact with Nina much earlier than others. For a long time, he loves Nina but cannot express his feelings to her. The cause behind his silence is his conception of love and his deep attachment with his mother. His indifferent attitude towards sex and his hidden love affairs keep him apart from others. For Nina, he is "womanless" and a "slack bachelor." Disclosing the cause of his bachelorhood, he admits : "You were my only true love, Nina, I made a vow of perpetual bachelorhood when you threw me over in Sam's favor" (p. 377). But he has no courage to disclose his inner feelings from the beginning. His idea of love is different from Darrell's scientific approach. His is the Platonic love, as he passionately says :

> My love is finer then any she has known! I do not just for her! ...I would be content if our marriage should be purely the placing of our ashes in the same tomb...Our urn side by side and touching one another...could the others say as much, could they love so deeply! (p. 406).

This illusory concept changes after the death of his mother, who is the only companion in his lonely life, and who has strong influence on him. Undoubtedly, Marsden loves Nina, but his love for Nina is suppressed by his real love for his mother. His work as a novelist, his friendships, his travels and all the major events in his life are governed by the dominant will of his mother. Naturally, he becomes helpless after her death. He says :

> ...and I have nothing!...but utter loneliness.. If only mother had lived! ...how horribly I miss her!... My lonely home...who will keep house for me now? (p. 376).

Marsden's solitary suffering and his long waiting come to an end, breaking his last illusion, with Nina's offer of marriage. Contrary to his conception, he has always been fascinated by her physical beauty; but now he gets a shattered, completely broken and an elderly women to look after her as a guardian. Finally, he accepts the truth with a tone of reconciliation :

> My life is cool green shade wherein comes no scorching zenith sun of passion and possession to wither the heart with bitter poisons...My life gathers roses, cooly crimison, in sheltered gardens, on late afternoons in love with evening...roses heavy with after blooming of the long day, desiring evening...My life is an evening...Nina is a rose, My rose, exhausted by the long, hot day, leaning wearily towards peace (pp. 438-39).

The other two characters who suffer isolation are Mrs. Evans, the mother of Sam, and Gordon Evans, the authorised son of Sam. Mrs. Evans spends a lonely life in order to save her son from the family curse. She narrates the story of her suffering to Nina as how she is forced to play the role of an alien mother to her only son. Her tragic alienation is expressed when she says : "I never let him come home...I was making him forget he had a mother" (p. 333). In the case of Gordon Jr., the isolation is of a different type. He remains unknown to his real identity. His real paternity acquires a mystery when we realize that "biologically" he is the son of Darrell, "spiritually" he is the son of Gordon Shaw, and "morally" he is the son of Sam Evans. Above all, sam Evans, who has enjoyed a normal life, does not know the falsity of his life that he is an alien son to his mother, alien husband to his wife, and alien father to his son.

Through these characters O'Neill successfully represents the predicament of a generation and the causes of the sickness of the modern times. It deals with the very problem of existence in the face of annihilating forces of a dark tradition that offers only an escape from reality and a dead past that spreads its sinister shadows into the present and chokes all the life out of it. The play presents life as a suspension bridge, "a strange interlude between unknown sinister past and the unexplored and unknown future."[13] It reveals the tragic consequences of the suppression of the basic urge of life through the characters of Prof. Leeds, Nina, Marsden,

Darrell, Sam, Mrs. Evans and Gordon, as "All of them live in a world of masks of the self and others"[14] The root-cause of their suffering is their romantic imagination, a disease owing to which they suffer from estrangement and become alienated from one another.

The title of the play, *Strange Interlude,* also evokes the theme of alienation. It is twice mentioned in the text. On the first occasion, Nina sees the barrenness of the present moment, a strange interlude between memory and expectation that becomes the cause of her isolation. On the second occasion, at the end she sees the whole of life like that — a mere interval between an unknowable past and future in which she and her dreams have no existence. As far the dramatic technique is concerned, O'Neill's use of monologue serves the function of mask in as much as it shows the gulf between a character's thought and his open words. Inner thoughts reveal the real feelings of a character — love, hatred or disgust. This device allows the playwright a freer hand to plumb into the continuous fluctuations going on in the minds of his characters. In this sense, 'asides are modified 'monologues.' The characters in the play reveal their true self with the help of 'monologues.' Asides,' which are heard by the audience but not by other characters, create an atomosphere of secrecy. They help the audience to understand the true motives of the characters and their duality.

4. *MOURNING BECOMES ELECTRA* (1931)

Mourning Becomes Electra (1931), one of the greatest tragedies of the twentieth century, depicts the story of man's unending suffering for the saks of search for identity. It proudly proves O'Neill's artistic craftsmanship as a playwright, and his power to tell a story superbly. Praising the play, B.H. Clark observes : "O'Neill's triology is a tearless tragedy, remote, detached, angst, artifully shaped, cunningly devised, skillfully related and magnificently conceived."[15] Through this triology, O'Neill expresses his concern not only for the evils of Puritanism but also for the evils of war, man's quest for beauty, and his wish to belong. It also shows how man fails to achieve these ends; he finds himself in a miserable condition to justify his existence, and is compelled to remain as an alienated person.

For presenting man's helplessness in the modern world, O'Neill has partially borrowed its plot from the famous Greek tragedy *Oresteia*. Like the Aeschylean tragedy, *Mourning Becomes Electra* Consists of three plays — 'Home Coming,' 'The Hunted,' and 'The Haunted.' In a letter to Robert Sisk, O'Neill clarifies :

> It is founded — in the outline plot — on the old story of Agamemnon, Clytemnestra, Electra, Orestes on which the Greek dramatist wrote triology. I modernize this story to a psychological drama of human interrelationships, using no Gods or heroes and interpret it with many variations and improvisations of my own.[16]

Though some of the important elements have been borrowed from the Greek story, they are presented in a modern form by the dramatist. The moral preoccupation of the Greek tragedian. Commensurate with the social, political and religious values of the contemporary Greece, has been replaced by the eternal struggle of man against external forces and his ultimate groping in the darkness of his own guilty self. However, the Greek concept of fate has been translated in terms of modern experience, where fate means man's personal, familiar and racial past and the forces of heredity and environment. In spite of its similarity with the Greek tragedy, it remains a modern play, treating the fundamental problems of the time in terms of modern values.

This story of isolation and separation is rooted in Mannon's family much before the beginning of the play. David Mannon, the uncle of Ezra, loved Marie Brantome, a girl below their rank. When she was pregnant, Abe Mannon brother of David, forced him to marry the girl and drove them out of the house. Abe grew rich; Ezra inherited his property; the poor Marie had to face starvation and death; and her son Adam Brant resolved to wreak vengeance upon Ezra. Ezra has had a glorious career, he joined army, gave it up, established a shipping firm, studied law, became a judge, joined politics and was elected Mayor, and when the American Civil War broke out, he again joined Army.

When the play opens the American Civil War has ended and General Ezra Mannon is about to return home to his wife, Christine, and daughter, Lavinia. Lavinia adores him, and is jealous of his affection for her mother. When she discovers the illicit affair between Adam Brant and her mother, she seeks to avenge her father by turning the family against her mother. When Ezra comes home, Christine, who has never loved him, poisons him, hoping to escape from the Mannon family with her lover Caption Brant. Orin, Lavinia's brother, who has been considered as Mama's boy returns just after death of his father. Lavinia tells him of Christine's unfaithfulness and of the suspected murder of General Mannon, who is suspected to have died of a heart-attack. In a fit of jealousy, Orin kills Brant in his ship, and his mother shoots herself. Orin then realizes that he has irrevocably lost his mother's love and, consumed by guilt, edges close to madness. In order to get rid of the gloomy surroundings of Mannon's castle, Lavinia and Orin go for a long sea-voyage in search of mental peace. After the long sea-voyage, Lavinia has the emotionally twisted Orin under her control. He, in turn, is insanely jealous and possessive of his sister. When Lavinia tries to involve with Peter, he threatens to expose their past, and commits suicide. Peter deserts Lavinia, who is left alone to let the past haunt her until the Mannon-curse is over. The problem of isolation is closely related to the loss of security and quest for one's happiness. All the major characters of this poignant tragedy suffer from the sense of insecurity, through they belong to a single family. It seems that all of them are living a life without any sense of relatedness with others. Ezra Mannon, the senior member of the family, is haunted by the same sense of isolation. Like all the Mannons, he has a mask-like look which symbolizes the split of his life. Outwardly, he is a successful man in every respect, but inwardly he is a helpless personal entirely cut-off from the marital bliss. He is hated by his wife owing to his Puritanic attitude : a common characteristic of the Mannons. In his life, he always seeks peace and happiness, tries to belong to somebody, but fails miserably. His longing for love is marred by the indifferent attitude of his wife. In search of belongingness when he returns home after the end of War, he finds himself in the same state of loneliness. He says : "I can't get used to home yet. It is so lonely."[17] He admits to his wife that "there'd always been some barrier between us — a wall hiding us from each other! I would try to make up my mind exactly what that wall was but I never could discover" (p. 54). It clearly shows that he is an alien husband to his wife.

After his marriage, he is haunted by a sense of nothingness that makes him a different man. He says : "...something keeps me sitting numb in my own Heart — like a statue of a dead man in a town square" (p. 55). Being dissatisfied with his wife, he turns to his daughter in search of peace which creates another barrier between the mother and the daughter. His joining of Mexican War after his marriage and his engagement in various business is the result of his wife's negation. Mocking at his achievement in life, he admits that the real reason behind his success in business is not his capability but his desire to be free from the isolated atmosphere of his home.

To bridge the gap, finally, he wants to surrender himself to the arms of his wife, but, to his ill-luck, he fails to find any thread of belongingness. Realizing the reality of their relation, he says to his wife in a bitter tone :

> Is that your notion of love? Do you think
> I married a body?...You were lying to me tonight

> as you've always lied! You were only pretending love! You made me appear a lustful beast in my own eyes! As you've always done since our first marriage night! I would feel cleaner now if I had gone to a brothel! I would feel more honor between myself and life! (p. 60).

But this in not the final relization; to his great amazement and horror, Christine tells him, before giving him the poison, instead of medicine, that she loves Adam Brant. Thus, a brave warrior like him dies a treacherous death plotted by his own wife.

The suffering of Christine Mannon is something different from that of her husband. She suffers not for the Puritanic attitude but for her sensuality and possessiveness. Rather, she is a rebel against the Puritanism of Mannons. In search of security, she marries Ezra. But, instead of getting a loving husband, she finds a cold-hearted person in him. She feels that her marriage with him quite unfortunate. As she is traditionally passionate due to her French origin, she cannot be able to adjust with her Puritanic husband. Soon, her marriage turns romance into disgust, and she is separated from her husband mentally. She accuses her husband : "You've used me, you've given me children, but I've never once been yours" (p. 61). Her longing for a happy life stops its breath under the Puritanic atmosphere of Mannon. Neglected by her husband, she gradually turns towards her son, Orin, to fill the vacuum. But she again finds herself in the same state of loneliness after his joining the army. She has lost her motherly affections towards her daughter and considers her as a competitor in the war of possession. She accuses Lavinia : "You've tried to become the wife of your father and the mother of Orin! You've always schemed to steal my place" (p. 33). This hostility reaches the climax when Lavinia discovers her mother's illicit relation with Adam Brant. Christine's with Brant is the result of her loneliness that arises due to the absence of Orin. She confesses : "I never would have fallen in love with Adam if I'd had Orin with me" (p. 32). She wants to go away from the house of Mannon through Brant, leaving all the sufferings behind. In search of happiness and 'belonging', she kills her husband and betrays her son, but finally fails to attain that. After the murder to Adam by Orin, she loses both her lover and her son. Her dream of a happy life and her desire of possession are shattered by the well-managed plan of Lavinia. She commits suicide to end her lonely life.

Another character who suffers from isolation and loneliness is Orin Mannon. Destiny has provided a bitter life to him. Throughout his life he remains a puppet in the hands of Christine and Lavinia. After feeling disgusted with Ezra when Christine turns towards him, he becomes an alien son to his father. As Christine says : "He hated you because he knew I loved you better than anything in the world (p. 86). Actually, Orin's mother-fixation is the root cause of his disillusionment. His strong attachment with his mother symbolises his longing for peace and security. While away at war, Orin dreamed of his mother as an island of peace :

> Those Island came to mean everything...that was peace and warmth and security. I used to dream I was there...There was no one there but you and me. And Yet I never saw you...I only felt you around me. The breaking of the waves was your voice. The sky was the same colour as your eyes. The warm sand was like your skin. The whole island was you (p. 90).

But, contrary to his dream, he finds himself in a strange atmosphere created by his mother and sister, Orin's arrival marks the beginning of the struggle between Christine and Lavinia. Each, tries to win him over to her side by showing him extra-sympathy and loyality. Each tries to poison his mind against the other. His sense of security and his dream of happy island shatter when Lavinia proves his mother's adultery.

Disappointedly he says : "I should never have come back to life — from my island of peace...But that is lost now" (p. 101). Out of jealousy he shoots Adam Brant on account of which Christine commits suicide. From this point onwards Orin leads a life of suffering and disillusionment. The memory of his dead mother haunts him. He feels himself guilty of the suicide of his mother. Being trapped by Lavinia's possessiveness, he tries to fulfil his desire for the mother and is ready to share the burden of guilt. He feels that neither he nor Lavinia have a right to love. He realizes :

> The only love I can know now is the love of guilt for guilt which breeds more guilt — until you get so deep at the botton of hell there is no lower you can sink and you rest there in peace (p. 160).

Gradually, he reaches a state of insanity that arises from his sense of guilt. He accuses Lavinia of being responsible for the mother's suicide, and suggests that they should confess and atone to the full extent of law : "That's the only way to wash the guilt of our mother's blood from our souls" (p. 152). Orin's deep attachment with Lavinia is nothing but the same quality of love and loathing for oneself that has always dominated Mannon-relationships. Orin hates Lavinia as much as he likes her. He does not like that she should marry Peter and threatens her to discolse the crime committed by them. Realizing the reality of Lavinia, he tells her : "There are times now when you don't seem to be my sister, nor mother, but some stranger" (p. 165). Finally, his guilt compels him to commit suicide like his mother, so that he may be able to regain his 'lost-island.'

The theme of isolation is aptly projected through the character of Lavinia Mannon, the modern Electra whose action dominates the play from the beginning to the end. Torn between the Puritanic father and the sensuous mother, she is haunted by a sense of loneliness throughout her life. She desperately wants to merge with the identity of her father, but finds her mother as a rival. She is the product of a disgusted romance of her parents. She feels :

> So I was born of your disgust : I've always guessed that, Mother — ever since I was little when — I used to come to you — with love — but you would always push me away : I've felt it ever since I can remember — your disgust : (p. 31).

Her alien childhood is the result of her mother's negation and her father — orientation. She is not only cut-off from her mother, but also separated from her brother. As Orin says : "he (father) always sided with you against Mother and me" (p. 97). In spite of her difference with her mother, she unconsciously feels that vacuum. She says "Oh mother" Why have you done this to me? "What harm have I done You?" (p. 57). On account of this atmosphere of hatred Lavinia has lost all the warm feelings of life. She becomes ruthless "cold and calm as an icicle" (p. 98).

Deprived of mother's love, she is deeply attached with her father and is in search of security which begins to crumble by the interference of Adam Brant. With all her efforts, she tries to keep her mother away from Brant for the reputation of her father. This makes the relations between the daughter and the mother bitter. Each tries to find some lame excuse to humiliate the other. Finally, the long-drawn war of possession for Ezra Mannon between Lavinia and Cristine ends with the death of Ezra. The death of her father is a terrible blow to her conception of security and belongingness for which she has been longing since her childhood. She is now haunted by same sense of loneliness again, and becomes more possessive. Her plan to snatch Orin for herself from her mother is the result of her insecurity, a common characteristic of Mannons. To get security and to keep Orin in her possession, Lavinia drives her brother first to kill Brant and then to drive Christine to commit suicide. But the death of Christine caused a new threat to her possession because Orin slowly drifts towards insanity. Both Lavinia and Orin are haunted by the sense of guilt. In order to be free from the haunted surroundings of the home, she plans for a sea-voyage. But her futile search for happiness again results in bitterness. They are constantly chased by the ghostly memory which compels them to return. Their own guilt divides them. Consequently both of them turn alien to each other in the haunted atmosphere of the house. She asks Orin : "But now you've suddenly become stranger again. You frighten me" (p. 41).

After returning from the voyage, Lavinia finds hereself in a terrible state of solitude. She turns colourless and looks like the ghost of her dead mother. Her possessiveness forces her to act like mother for Orin; and she tries to make him forgetful of his loss. She pleads to him to forget the past and to develop a more meaningful relationship with the immediate present. Even she hopes to mitigate the pain of isolation by marrying Peter. But she fails miserably in her attempt. She realizes that playing with human lives and human emotions is not a mechanical game with forseeable results. Comparing Lavinia with Nina of *Strange Interlude*, Harry Slochower states :

> In Nina and Lavinia, O Neill presents the ultimate in self and social alienation. Both are the masochistic products of modern rationalistic probing. Both attempt to wield and possess people's lives, as if they were "god and had created them." Nina renounces at the end. Lavinia remains defiant even in her acceptance of suffering.[18]

In spite of her excessive desire to fall in love with Peter, she rejects the proposal of marriage. She realizes that Mannons have no right to love or to be loved in this world. She has decided to spend the remaining days of her life in the isolated house of Mannons. Before entering the lonely cell, she says :

> I'm the last Mannon. I've got to punish myself

> Living alone here with the dead is a worse act of justice than death or prison : I'll never go out or see anyone : I'll have the shutters nailed closed so no sunlight can ever get in. I'll live alone with the dead.... (p. 178).

Lavinia, however, is made of different stuff Both Christine and Orin are cowards, cannot bear agonies, and cannot repent and expiate sin. Lavinia, on the contrary, has tragic heroism in her. In fact, she realizes the power of the curse working upon the Mannon family, and in order to get rid of it she thinks of paying for it. Therefore, she has surrendered herself to isolation and remains alienated for ever.

Though O'Neill has provided little space for Adam Brant, his involvement makes him an important character in the play. Destroying himself, he adds fuel to the isolated suffering of Mannons. His passion for revenge and his hatred towards Mannons provide him an isolated life. Being a Mannon, he is entirely cut-off from the family. He has been separated even from his parents. He says : "At seventeen I ran away to sea — and forgot I had a mother" (p. 26). He hates his father David Mannon because he was the man who loved his mother and left her in miserable condition. Instead of giving her a happy life, he made her life hell. For the same reason, he hates Ezra Mannon because the latter refused to help his starving mother after the death to David Mannon. By possessing Christine, he wanted to fulfil his desire for revenge, but during the course of possessing her, he became her possession. The other two characters, who suffer from separation, are Peter and Hazel. Their longing for love remains unfulfilled till the end. Neither Peter is united with Lavinia nor Hazel with Orin.

The title, setting and technique play an important role in revealing the theme of isolation an loneliness in the play. The title, "Mourning Becomes Electra," symbolizes alienation in a different way. Like the dual nature of his characters, the dramatist provides a double meaning to the title. O'Neill states : "It befits — it becomes Electra to mourn,"[19] and the second meaning has its ironical significance : "Mourning (black) is becoming to her — it is the only colour that becomes her destiny."[20] It clearly suggests the suffering of human beings in a state of loneliness which is justified through the character of Lavinia, the modern Electra. After the death of all the major characters, she is left alone to suffer in a state of wilderness. Even the sub-titles of the triology are symbolic. "Home Coming" symbolizes Ezra Mannon's search for belonging in his own home that has remained a strange place for him. Again, it symbolizes Christine's search for security in the arms of Adam Brant. "The Hunted" symbolizes man's condition in the society of perverted values. "The Hunted" symbolizes man's relation with his past which compulsively makes him an alienated person.

The setting of scenes in this play is well-planned, and explores and communicates the theme. The use of external and internal scenes becomes symbolic in the play. The external scenes indicate the chief characters, desire to escape into some land of peace, while the internal ones symbolize the suppression and denial of natural instinct to live. O'Neill's use of symbols and masks reveals the hidden desire of the characters. In this play, he uses mask-like faces instead of masks. Almost all the characters of this play have a 'mask-like face' which symbolically suggests their split, and inner disharmony. This mask-like face has created a barrier between the common people and the Mannons. The important symbols in the play, used by O'Neill, for exposing the theme of alienation are 'the house of Mannons,' 'the South Sea Island' and 'the song chanty Shenandoah.'

The House is characteristic of the Mannon family and its fate. It functions as a visual participant in the action of the play. The life within the house is in sharp contrast to the life outside it. The indoor life reveals hypocrisy, selfishness, isolation; and the outside life is quite attractive but terrifying. The contrast between the portico and the house is also suggestive. The white portico is suggestive of the mask that all Mannons wear the mask if isolation and secrecy —, while the house itself becomes a witness to seething Puritanical inhibitions, and to the dark deed of murder and suicide, of adultery and incest. It is the place of death and suffering, shutting out life like an outsider.

In contrast to 'the house of Mannons,' 'the South Sea Island' symbolizes the Mannons' longing for peace and security. The Mannons are separated from one another, and they have always haunted by a sense of insecurity. They search for identity because they are not able to belong to the ghostly atmosphere of their house. All of them long for the peace, security and innocence of the South Sea Islands. But in reality, the Islands are unattainable. The vision and the dream cannot be realized, and for the Mannons, there is no escape from complexes and illusions.

Another suggestive symbol used by O'Neill to explore the theme is 'the sea-chanty Shenandoah.' "Home Coming" opens with the song sung by Seth, the housekeeper of Mannons. The desire to put to sea — "the sailor is bound away across the wide Missouri" (p. 6) — results in frustration and separation, and "Oh, Shenandoah, I can't get near you" (p. 6) symbolises an unnavigable gulf. The song that recurs of Christine's suicide — "She's far away across the story water" (p. 124) — reveals that the separation is final. The stormy waters that separate man from his desire cannot be crossed except by the death. In the closing scene of the play, Seth mournfully sings the song as if to bid farewell to Lavinia for her unending journey of suffering.

REFERENCES

[1] Eugene O'Neill, *Nine Plays* (New York : Modern library, 1941), p. 136. Hereafter the quotes from *Desire Under the Elms* will refer to this edition and be indicated only by the page number in parenthesis in the body of this Study.

[2] Travis Bogard, *Contour in Time : Plays of O'Neill* (New York : Oxford Univ. Press, 1972), p. 221.

[3] Travis Bogard and Jackson R. Bryer, eds., *Selected Letters of Eugene O'Neill* (New Haven : Yale Univ. Press, 1980), p. 524.

[4] Eugene O'Neill, *The Great God Brown and Lazarus Laughed* (London : Jonathan Cape Ltd., 1960), p.11. Hereafter the quotes from *the Great God Brown* will refer to this edition and be indicated only by the page number in parenthesis in the body of this study.

[5] Quoted in Gelb, *O'Neill*, p. 580.

[6] *Ibid.*

[7] Quoted in Gelb, *O'Neill,* p. 580.

[8] Travis Bogard, *Contour in Time*, pp. 277-78.

[9] Arthur and Barbara Gelb, *O'Neill*, p. 629.

[10] Eugene O'Neill, *Selected Plays of Eugene O'Neill* (New York : Random House, 1967), p. 285. Hereafter the quotes from *Strange Interlude* will refer to this edition and be indicated only by the page number in parenthesis in the body of this study.

[11] *Selected Letters of Eugene O'Neill*, ed. Travis Bogard and Jackson R. Bryer (New Haven : Yale Univ. Press, 1988), p. 548.

[12] Clifford Leech, *O'Neill* (London : Oliver and Boyd Ltd., 1963), p. 79.

[13] S.K. Winter, *Eugene O'Neill : A Critical Study* (New York : Random House, 1961), p. 261.

[14] Doris V. Folk. *Eugene O'Neill and the Tragic Tension* (New Jersey : Rutgers Univ. Press, 1958), p. 126.

[15] B. H. Clark, *Eugene O'Neill : The Man and His Plays* (New York : Dover, 1947), p. 170.

[16] *Selected Letters of Eugene O'Neill,* p. 368.

[17] O'Neill, *The Plays of Eugene O'Neill* (New York : Random House, 1955), p. 54. Hereafter, the quotes from *Mourning Becomes Electra* will refer to this edition and be indicated only by the page number in parenthesis in the body of this study.

[18] Harry Slochower, "Eugene O'Neill's Lost Moderns," *O'Neill and His Plays*, ed. Cargil *et al.*, p. 386.

[19] Quoted in Sheaffer, *O'Neill : Son and Artist* (Boston : Little Brown Company, 1973), p. 338.

[20] *Ibid.*

4

The Later Phase

The chapter is devoted to the analysis of the four major plays of Eugene O'Neill, written during the last phase of his career; they are : *The Iceman Cometh* (1939), *Long Day's Journey into Night* (1941), *A Touch of the Poet* (1942) and *A Moon for the Misbegotten* (1942). In these highly autobiographical plays O'Neill portrays the most agonised picture of man. They deal with the characters, who sustain their survival on their broken dreams which breed a sense of isolation and loneliness — the most dangerous pest, consuming mankind. All these plays are the results of the personal anguish and desperation of the dramatist. As Doris V. Falk observes :

> O'Neill returned in these last plays to acceptance of struggle and flight as inseparable from and intrinsic to life process. Now there is no way out but death. The struggle in these plays is essentially the same as it had always been in his work : the conscious intellect at war with the unconscious drives, the laceration of love and hate in every close human relationship, and the desperate search for self among the masks.[1]

These beautiful pieces of dramatic art are born out of agony and ecstasy that mark the culmination of O'Neill's dramatic career.

One of the most striking qualities of all these plays is the huge quantity of alcohol consumed by the characters in each of them. Liquor in these plays serves a double function. It permits the playwright to show the contrast between a man when he is sober with his defences up and when he is drunk making his subconscious drives overt. The playwright allows the rapid juxtaposition of contradictory moods and impulses. It is a device through which O'Neill exposes the real motives of his characters.

1. *THE ICEMAN COMETH* (1939)

The Iceman Cometh (1939) depicts the story of man's rootlessness and isolation in the modern world. It presents before us the intensely human and vital drama of the tragic and deadly struggle between man's illusions and the naked brutal realities of life. O'Neill personally considers that the play "is one of the best things I've ever done. In some way, perhaps *the* best."[2] Throughout his life O'Neill has tried to achieve dramatic unity between form and feeling, between thought and technique. His endeavor in this direction bears a nice fruit in this play. Analyzing the play, Rosamond Gilder opines :

> *The Iceman Cometh* is made of good theatre substance — meaty material for actors, racy dialogue, variety of character, suspense and passion — all within the strait-jacket of a rigid pattern. It is also primarily an allegory of man's pitiful estate, a parable of his search for redemption.[3]

The play deals simply and grandly with the illusion and disillusion of a group of men in an archetypal bar and their tragic suffering from separation.

The action of the play takes place in Harry Hope's Saloon and rooming-house in Westside, New York. The Saloon is occupied by a number of derelicts who indulge themselves and each other in dreams of former and future glory. Life becomes bearable for them only because each of them has his own illusion or pipe-dream either about the past or the future.

In this way, each of the 'bums' lives in a golden yesterday or a golden tomorrow, forgetful of his wretched present. Among them is the testy but soft-hearted owner himself who has not set his foot outdoors for twenty years. He lives under the illusion that he loved his wife, and that her death, twenty years ago, robbed his life of all its charms. His two permanent roomers and friends are Pat McCloin, an ex-police officer who hopes to get back his job some day, and Ed Mosher, an ex-circusman, who thinks that he can go back to his job any day he likes. There are also General Wetjeon, a Dutch, and Captain Lewis, an Englishman, who had fought on opposite sides in the Boer War. Both of them believe that they will work, save enough, and go back to their respective countries. Joe Mott, a negro, the ex-owner of a gambling house, hopes to start a new gambling-house in near future. Hugo and Larry are the two ex-anarchists. Hugo is never sober and talks constantly about the Revolution which will enable him to drink champagne under the willow tree. Larry's illusion is that since he gave up the Movement, he has been a disinterested observer of life, quietly waiting for death. He is disturbed by the arrival of young Don Parritt, whose mother has recently been denounced and arrested by other anarchists. Parritt insists on telling his problems to Larry, who gets increasingly uneasy and does not want to become involved with Parritt. Jimmy Tomorrow, the ex-news-reporter, always plans to give up drinking, and hopes to get his old job tomorrow. Willie Oban, a Harvard Law School graduate, dreams of becoming a successful lawyer one day. There are also Chuck and Rocky, the bartenders, who think that they are not pimps; and the three street-walkers, Cora, Pearl and Margie, who confess to be tarts but not whores.

All the characters are guilt-ridden due to their ruined lives, and all cling to pipe-dreams about their condition and the future. They are eagerly awaiting the entertaining and generous Hickey, a travelling salesman, who periodically treats them in a lavish manner. When Hickey finally arrives in time for Harry's birth day, they are shocked to find him greatly changed. He announces that he has finally had the courage to face himself and to lay his pipe-dreams to rest. Further, he intends to help others do the same for their own happiness. But to his anticipation, he finds that his gospel of disillusionment does not work. He is forced to explain the cause of his reform in order to prove his statements. He narrates the story of his life, his relations with his innocent wife, Evelyn, who for all the years of their marriage had invariably forgiven his drinking and infidelities. He tells that in order to free her from the torment of his presence, he killed her. But soon he realizes that this too was an illusion because he killed her out of hatred. Parritt also admits that he betrayed his mother out of hatred. Both, in effect, destroyed their lives : Hickey by summoning police, Parritt by committing suicide. The idea that Hickey is insane gradually develops as a new pipe-dream, allowing the others to resume their old relationships and illusions; and only Larry, who perceives Hickey as the Iceman of Death, remains truly and despairingly in a state of isolation.

All the characters of the play are drawn from the people whom O'Neill had personally known during his New York days. Even the setting is made of details taken from the places with which O'Neill was personally familiar. The description of Harry Hope's Saloon at the opening of the play reveals of alienated life of its occupants. The dismal atmosphere with dirty floor and walls with crumbling plaster narrate the desolate condition of the bums. For them, Hope's Saloon is their ultimate destination, their limitation, from where they cannot go. It is the Saloon which separates them from society, severes them from their deadly past, and forces them to lead a life of isolation. But in a state of illusion, they consider the place as the safest one where they can dream their golden tomorrow. As Larry says to Parritt :

> Don't you notice the beautiful calm in the atmosphere? That's because it's the last harbor.

> No one here has to worry about where they're going next, because there is no farther they can go.[4]

The derelicts of the saloon are separated from the normal life of society. Without facing the reality, they have taken shelter in the illusory world of Harry Hope's Saloon and remain isolated from the outer world. The dreamers have come to Hope's Saloon in search of security and happiness because what lies outside is a world without values, a hostile society to which they can hardly belong. But this is not the reality; rather it is an escape from the truth. In this connection, Brooks Atkinson remarks :

> But beneath them there is nothing more substantial than a void of blackness. These are creatures that once were men — very pungent and picturesque creatures, too, for O'Neill was a good deal of a romantic... Life is bearable, it seems to say, only when men contrive not to look at the truth.[5]

The greatest irony of their lives is that in search of belongingness they are alienated from the reality of life.

With the interference of Hickey, they begin to accept the truth and admit their suffering from isolation. Harry, the generous bar-owner, narrates the story of his lonely life. It begins with the death of his wife. He recalls :

> Twenty years, and I've never set foot out of this house since the day I buried her. Didn't have the heart. Once she'd gone, I didn't give a damn for anything. I lost all my ambition. Without her, nothing seemed worth the trouble (p. 645).

The haunting memory of his wife keeps him apart from the outer world. But Jimmy's lonely suffering is the result of his wife's betrayal. His longing for a happy home is shattered by the dishonesty of his wife. In order to mitigate the pain of separation, he prefers to lead a gloomy life taking drinks as his lonely companion.

Their discussion with each other reveals the cause of their suffering. Living a life of tramps in a cheap hotel, they are separated from one another in several ways. Joe, the negro, hates Rocky because he is a white boy. Living among the white people, he has lost his sense of belongingness and has developed a guilty complex. When he decides to leave the place, he says : "I's goin' to my own folks where I belong" (p. 708). Similarly, when Cora and Chuck decide to marry and leave the place, Rocky mocks at him. His mocking is nothing but the jealously of love towards Chuck. Chuck accuses : "Yuh don't wanta see me get married and settle down like a reg'lar guy!" (p. 706).

Realizing the reality through Hickey's speech, the bums decide to leave the place in search of happiness. His gospel has a tremendous impact on them. Even Hugo, who has been searching peace through drinks under the willow tree, finds it difficult to get it. Out of disgust he utters : "Life is a crazy monkey-face! Always there is blood beneath the willow trees! I hate it and I am afraid!" (p. 728). But this realization does not last long. The illusion clouds over the truth when Hickey confesses his murdering of his wife. The hope of the bums shatters again; they finally return to the Sallon, which would keep them away from the reality of life.

Apart from the secondary characters, the three chief figures of the play, who suffer from the sense of isolation, are Hickey, Larry and Parritt. Hickey becomes the victim of isolation due to his fickle nature and his falsity. Since his childhood he has been restless and reckless, desiring change. His home, his school and his town appear to him like prisons. His father is a clergy whom he admires and from whom he acquires the smoothness in talking to people. But he is separated from his father by choosing the profession of salesmanship. Early in life, he moves in the company of tarts who like him for his entertaining jokes. He is already in love with Evelyn, and when he runs away from home, she promises to wait till he is successful and is in a position to marry her and support the family. To seek his fortune, he leaves home and his father, and is separated himself from his family.

The profession chosen by Hickey, causes his separation from his wife and is also responsible for his solitary life. In order to mitigate the pain of separation, he finds consolation in the company of girls and in drinking. As he is devoted to Evelyn, he confesses everything to her, and each time she forgives him. She pardons him even when he catches a venereal disease and transfers it to her. This makes him feel very guilty. In his anguished soul, he feels that he is doing great wrong to the sweetest innocent that has ever lived, and yearns for some way to make her contented and at peace. He examines various possibilities, such as suicide, running away from home, etc., but comes to the conclusion that in this way he would cause her even greater pain.

He does not give up his periodic drinks, and she can not help forgiving even his worst sins. She is always in a state of illusion; her loyalty for Hickey is merely a pipe-dream, which she never avoids. The situation becomes intolerable and a sense of guilt constantly haunts him. He says :

> God, can you picture all I made her suffer, and all the guilt she made me feel, and how I hated myself.... (p. 745).

The love-hate relationship between Hickey and Evelyn make Hickey a split personality, an isolated figure. He expresses his tragic suffering in these words :

> ...I loved her so, but I began to hate that pipe dream! I began to be afraid I was going....forgive her for forgiving me... and it made me hate myself all the more... I'd get so damned lonely.... (p. 746).

In a state of illusion he decides to kill her in order to ease his guilty conscience. But after killing Evelyn he realizes the truth. Instead of killing her out of love and mercy, he kills her out of hate.

As Hickey realizes his failure, he welcomes his doom. Death will be the only solution of his suffering and pipe-dream. What he has regarded as peace and contentment is nothing but an illusion and the only cause of his solitary suffering. After his confession, Larry remarks : "May the Chair bring him peace at last, the poor tortured bastard!" (p. 750).

Larry Slade, the ex-anarchist, the chief exponent of O'Neill's philosophy of life in this play, is also a victim of isolation. Throughout the play he pretends complete detachment and disinterestedness, but he is unable to forget his past. His pipe-dream is that he has lost all interest in life and is simply waiting for death. Through him O'Neill suggests the way to achieve happiness. Life is endured only with the aid of pipe-dream and wine. Deprived of these, men begin to die. But once they are reconciled to death, it, too, brings peace.

Being separated from the mainstream of life, Larry takes shelter under the gloomy atmosphere of Harry Hope's Saloon, and considers it as his last resort. As an ex-anarchist, once he had great faith in the Movement, but he left it because he quarrelled with Rosa Parritt, the woman whom he loved so dearly. Rosa Parritt was always a strong supporter of the Movement. On the other hand Larry realized that the Movement was a futile search, a mere pipe-dream for him. He was disillusioned with the human material with which he had to work.

Separated from Rosa Parritt, he emerges with another pipe-dream — *viz.*, he has forgotten the past. In a way, he is alienated from the reality because he does not care for the truth. He says :

> To hell with the truth! ... the truth has no bearing on anything. It's irrelevant and immaterial... The lie of a pipe dream is what gives life to the whole misbegotten mad lot of us, drunk or sober (p. 623).

In order to avoid the truth, he keeps himself apart from the reality and prefers to stay in a state of illusion. He believes that he does not have any pipe-dreams. He replies to Rocky : "Mine are all dead and buried behind me" (p. 624). He even denies his previous pipe-dream of anarchist movement that has separated him from his beloved and compelled him to lead a solitary life.

Frustrated and disillusioned, he thinks that he has forgotten the past, but the past confronts him in the person of Don Parritt, the son of Rosa Parritt. At first, he denies his intimacy with her and considers the affair as a common matter. He says to Don Parritt :

> I never answered her last letters. I haven't written her in a couple of years — or any one else.' I've gotten beyond the desire to communicate with the world — or, what's more to the point, let it bother me any more with its greedy madness (p. 633).

It clearly shows how he is separated from the outer world, having no relation with others. The reason of Larry's alien life is his separation from the Movement, and he reveals it :

> If I don't believe in the Movement, I don't believe in anything else either, especially not the state. I've refused to become a useful member of its society (p. 634).

His concept begins to change, and he reveals that he still loves Rosa and has some faith in the great cause. This faith is finally shattered when Parritt commits suicide, and he becomes a real convert to death. He pathetically confesses :

> Be God, there is no hope! I'll never be a success in the grand stand — or anywhere else! Life is too much for me! I'll be a weak fool looking with pity at the two sides of everything till the day I die.... (p. 757).

The split in his character is the main cause of his tragic suffering emanating from isolation. Larry considers that he is an objectivist — one who sees both sides of the picture — and thus tries to reach the truth. But too much of thinking makes him a paralysed spectator, who is unable to take action in any direction. The two sides he sees are the masks of his own self, and both the selves are illusory, unreal and worthless. As Doris V. Falk opines :

> If Larry had been able to give either of these selves the value of a reality, he would have been drawn toward one or toward the other, would have been able to act either in the direction of his political obligations or in the direction of death by suicide, as Parritt did. Since he is pulled in both directions at once, he can only withdraw from the struggle altogether and become a non-participating observer of himself as well as of life.[6]

Man's search for security and loss of belongingness in the modern world are projected through the character of Don Parritt in the play. Being detached from the 'Movement' and his mother, he comes to Larry in the hope of seeking security. His appearance and manner keep him apart from the other bums of Harry Hope's Saloon. He does not find the Saloon an interesting place. He likes neither the Saloon, nor does he identify himself with the occupants of the Saloon. Even the birthday party of Harry hardly matters to him. He says : "I don't belong in this birthday celebration. I don't know this gang and I don't want to be mixed up with them" (p. 683). As he has no father, he becomes insecure and helpless after the imprisonment of his anarchist mother. He speaks of his lonely childhood as how he passes a solitary life without the love of a mother and without a friend.

Parritt's cause of suffering from isolation is his betrayal of nature. He betrays his own mother and becomes the cause of her imprisonment. He first pretends that he did so out of patriotism, for he did not want his country to be ruined by a foreign pipe-dream. But he soon confesses that this was not his real motive. He betrays her because he wants money to spend somewhere. His motive is mercenary. But this, too, soon turns out to be a lie. He soon admits that he did not betray her for money. The real reason was that he did not like her free ways. He says : "She just had to keep on having lovers to prove to herself how free she was... It made home a lousy place. I felt like...it was like living in a whorehouse" (p. 685).

Thus, in order to get rid of the ill-atmosphere of home, he betrayed his mother out of hate. In this respect his case runs closely parallel to the case of Hickey. Apropos of thus, Edwin A. Engel opines :

> Hickey's wife and Parritt's mother represent antithetical aspects of love — the former an excess of love and forgiveness, the latter a deficiency. Both generate hate in the men who are closely associated with them.[7]

Indeed, he is the worse sinner of the two, for he has sent his mother to jail. In this regard, Parritt reminds us of Orin Mannon of *Mourning Becomes Electra*. Both are lonely, and are haunted by a sense of guilt. But in the case of Orin, he loves his mother whereas Parritt hates his.

Like Orin, Parritt suffers from a haunting sense of guilt. It is this guilt-complex which makes him nervous, shy, reserved and suspicious. The mother-image constantly haunts him and he feverishly seeks a way out for his spiritual troubles. He cannot take any decision by himself, for his mother always dominated him and decided things for him. He wants some guide or mentor, some one to show him the way out of his troubles. At last, through Larry he finds the way. He commits suicide like that of Orin Mannon to make an end of his lonely suffering.

The play dramatizes the relationship between men's illusion

and their will to live. It deals with one of the most crucial problems of man's flight from reality into the realm of illusion. The world of reality has nothing to offer to the bums, and there is no place for such shirkers and idlers in it. The world of reality is a symbol of constant terror for them, and they cannot belong to it in an honorable manner. Thus, in a state of illusion they dream for the tomorrow that keeps them isolated from today's reality of life.

2. *LONG DAY'S JOURNEY INTO NIGHT* (1941)

Long Day's Journey into Night (1941) is the most personal of O'Neill's plays. It is a simple naturalistic family drama without any plot contrivance, but is remarkable for its uncommonly moving revelation of characters and human relations. The elegiac but harrowing portrayal of a family's love-hate conflicts places this play among O'Neill's greatest works.

The play deals with the inter-family isolation and shows how an outwardly prosperous and happy family suffers from isolation. O'Neill exhibits unique courage in revealing his personal and private life in it. It really goes to his credit that he has turned autobiography into a play with sufficient objectivity.

The play opens in Tyrones's fogbound summer house which keeps them apart from the outer world and the present reality of life. It depicts the story of four Tyrones, the money-loving father, James Tyrone, his wife Mary, their elder son, Jamie, and the younger son, Edmund. As the play proceeds, it reveals the inner story of the family and the suffering of its members from isolation and separation.

Mary, who has just returned from a mental hospital, makes clear by her attitude that she is not cured. She nostalgically revives her past dreams of becoming a nurse or a pianist, and appears to be an innocent girl once again. She also reveals that her addiction began when her miserly husband chose a quack-doctor who treated her after her sickness in giving birth to Edmund with morphine. Like her mother, Edmund wants to move away from reality, and prefers to stay alone. Like her, he, too, shows both love and hate for his family as he confronts his limited future as a consumptive, realizing that since he is expected to die, his father will send him to the cheapest state sanitorium. A similar ambivalence is exhibited by the debauched Jamie, who drunkenly tells Edmund how much he loves him and yet how much he hates him as he (Edmund) is responsible for their mother's addiction. Both Edmund and Jamie accuse their father of the destruction of the family. In defence, James Tyrone tells the story of his tragic childhood that taught him the value of money. Each member of the family confronts his own failure and guilts, which end in frustration and futility. In the end, we witness Mary's special fascination for the past and her unhappiness about the present.

The theme of isolation and loneliness is projected through all the major characters in the play. All of them are suffering from a deep sense of isolation. James Tyrone leads an estranged life owing to his materialistic attitude and his profession. In his search for monetary security, he is hated by his wife and sons. The tragic irony of his life is that he remains a stranger to his family for which he has sacrificed his life. By choosing the profession of an actor, he has spent most of his time in cheap hotels and bars, and has never provided a comfortable life to his wife and children. His indifferent attitude proves too much to his family and separates him from his wife. Out of disgust, his wife remarks :

> Oh, I'm so sick and tired of pretending this is a home! You wan't help me... You don't know how to act in home! You don't really want one!... never since the day we were married! You should have remained a bachelor and lived in second-rate hotels and entertained your friends in bar-rooms![8]

He fails to prove himself a worthy husband to his wife. His incapability of providing a real home makes him a stranger.

His wife says, "It's hard for a stranger to tell, but after thirty-five years of marriage" (p. 71). Not only from his wife, his materialistic attitude also separates him from his sons. His elder son Jamie has the same opinion about him. When James prefers to Edmund to Dr. Hardy, a cheap doctor, for the treatment, Jamie redicules his father. He says, "Hardy only charges a dollar. That's what makes you think he's a fine doctor!" (p. 26). Everybody accuses him, but nobody changes his concept of doctor. As his tragic childhood taught him the worth of a dollar, he always feels insecure by remembering the penniless days of his early life. His wife remarks :

> And Mr. Tyrone is never worried about anything, except money and property and the fear he'll end his days in poverty. I mean, deeply worried. Because he cannot really understand anything else (p. 87).

It is his monetary insecurity that keeps him apart from others, and compels him to live a life of stranger in his own family.

Although his search for economic security and his fear of poor house make him stingy, he honours the bound of the home more than any other member of the family. He shoulders the responsibilities of their lives more than any other member of his family. He is capable of love, but is often driven towards hatred. Even then, he never truly hates any of his family members, but lives isolated within the frame of the bond, attempting to love all. His failure as an artist and a husband creates a vacuum within him. He turns from the pain of his life to the local bar-room, and drinks to dope his mind to the point of forgetfulness. He remains a lonely man, free of cynicism and incapable of hatred.

Mary Tyrone is the most unfortunate person who suffers from a deep sense of alienation. In search of happiness, she has married Tyrone, rejecting her dreams and ambitions of innocent girlhood by becoming a nun or a concert pianist. Her dreams shatter when she falls in love with James. At the time of her marriage, she thinks of herself as the happiest women of the world; but soon she begins to feel that there is no happiness for her. Being an actor's wife, she has to travel with her husband on his road-tours and stay in cheap hotels. This deprives her of a real home and makes her an alien wife. Her husband prefers to stay in clubs or bar-rooms, and she feels terribly lonely. In the dirty hotels, she has to wait for her husband alone, as she is unable to associate herself with theater-people and has to spend night in idleness until her husband comes or is brought home from the theater. Her sense of isolation and loneliness increases when she finds that she cannot communicate with the outer world. She says : "There is no-where I could go. Who would I go to see? I have no friends" (p. 72). For this, she accuses her husband and blames him for his indifferent attitude towards a real home. She feels that she has married beneath her status, and that she is unable to go out and meet people. She cannot invite her friends since she has no permanent home. She never considers the summer-house a real home. Her conception of real home keeps her apart from the outer world and separates her from her family. She expresses her belief to her husband : "In a real home one is never lonely. You forget I know from my experience what a home is like. I gave up one to marry you — my father's home" (p. 62). Her longing for a real home is marred by the materialistic attitude of her husband, and has compelled her to lead a solitary life.

Being dissatisfied with the present, she moves towards the past in search of peace and security. She passionately remembers her thrilling convent days and her romantic affairs with James. She recollects her tragic experience and the life-and-death-struggle at the time of Edmund's birth. She cannot forget the cheap quack who prescribed her morphine to kill her pain, and thus made her a permanent drug-addict. She blames herself for causing the death of Edmund due to her sheer negligence and indifference. She realises that she has been a liar throughout her life, and has been false not only to others but also to herself. Thus, she remains isolated from the present.

Mary is constantly haunted by a sense of guilt. She does not consider herself a worthy mother, and for this she blames her husband. From her experience she knows : "Children should have homes to be born in, if they are to be good children, and women need home, if they are to be good mothers" (p. 76). Also, she blames herself for the cause of Edmund's ill health. She says, "He was born nervous and too sensitive, and that's my fault" (p. 76). Her failure as a good mother develops a sense of hatred within herself that keeps her apart from the rest of the family members. Accusing her husband, she says to Edmund :

> I know why we wants to send you to a Sanitorium. To take you from me! He's tried to do that. He's been jealous of everyone of my babies. He kept finding ways to make me leave them (p. 103).

Her hatred of Jamie is less ambiguous. She hates his cynicism, turns from him in fear that he will discover her need of the dope-dream, and silently accuses him of murdering the dead child. At the same time, she cannot help herself being in love with them. Her love-hate relationship with her family leave her in the alternate states of disillusion and illusion.

Her search for happiness through falsity keeps her away from others as well as from herself. Her self-deception and escapism are heightened by her constant reference to her glasses which she can never find. She says, "My eyes are getting so bad and I never can find my glasses" (p. 18). The search for the glasses signifies her search for identity, search for self that does not exist. It indicates her inability to see herself as she is. Actually, unable to find solace in the present, she moves backwards and isolates herself from the reality and from her true-self.

Through the character of Mary, O'Neill expresses his firm conviction that we are what life has made us, and that we are able to know its foul game only when it is too late to do anything about it. In her words :

> None of us can help the things life has done to us. They're done before you realize it, and once they're done they make you do other things until at last everything comes between you and what you'd like to be, and you've lost your true self forever (p. 53).

Haunted by an utter sense of loneliness and insecurity, she takes more and more of the drugs so that she may live in the past which is the only reality to her. She loves the fog since it hides her from the world of reality; but she hates the foghorn which reminds her of the harsh and nagging realities. At the end of the play, her appearance in the wedding gown is a symbol of her quest for hope and her longing for happiness which are never fulfilled.

Jamie, like the other members of his family, suffers from a sense of isolation and separation. He leads a meaningless life without any goal. He has the potentiality of becoming a fine actor, but with his perpetual alcoholism and whore-mongering, he blots out the possibility of becoming some prominent person in life. He becomes a wastrel and a cynic, sneering at everything but himself. He is a nagging son to his parents. He has a hostile relation with his father, for whom he is no more than a vagabond who does not know the value of money. His father blames him for his repeated failure in the job he does, and has lost his hopes on him. He also accuses him of the downfall of Edmund. He thinks that it is Jamie who has had a bad influence on his younger brother. Commenting on his cynical attitude, his father says :

> Your mind was so poisoned by your own failure in life, you wanted to believe every man was a knave with his soul for sale, and every woman who wasn't whore was a fool (p. 30).

His mother has the same opinion regarding his failure, but in a tone of consideration she says : "But I suppose life has made him like that, and he can't help it" (p. 53).

Jamie's malicious attitude towards Edmund reveals the main cause of his isolation. He hates Edmund because he is the root-cause of their mother's drug addiction. He thinks that Edmund has stolen the love of his mother and forced him to live a loveless life. Pointing out the cause of Jamie's failure and solitary suffering, Travis Bogard opines :

> Jamie, like his brother and father, is lost, embittered and cynical, wanting his mother whose rejection of his perhaps reaches farther back than the time when morphine forced her into drugged isolation.[9]

Deprived of mother's love and father's affection, he turns into a half-dead person. He feels that a part of himself has long been dead. He warns Edmund to be wary of him :

> Because I'll do my damned to make you fail. Can't help it. I hate myself. Got to take revenge. On everyone else. Especially you... The dead part of me hopes you won't get well. May be he's even glad the game has got Mama again. He wants company, he doesn't want to be the only corpse around the house.... (p. 146).

Love is the essential truth, a bare necessity for every human being. It helps him to lead a happy life, but when he fails to achieve it, he becomes frustrated and gets isolated. It happens in the life of Jamie. He pleads to Edmund : "Don't forget love. What a man without a good woman's love? A God-damned hollow shell" (p. 129). In his search for love, he visits whore-house, but he is not satisfied even there. In this regard, he reminds us of Dion Anthony of *The Great God Brown*. Both are the seekers of love, but there is a difference between them. In the case of Dion, Cybel is the substitute for his mother's love, while in the case of Jamie, Mary is not a perfect substitute.

Edmund, the younger son of Tyrones, is a victim of isolation and loss of belongingness. From the autobiographical point of view, he is the self-portrait of Eugene O'Neill. Through him the playwright recalls his own bitter past and the failure of his early years. Like him, O'Neill is also sick and sensitive. Each tries to interpret life from a very personal angle. Edmund is an embittered adolescent like the dramatist. Each suffers from the feeling of being unwanted even in his domestic circle.

Edmund leads a life of utter aimlessness and dissolution because he considers himself a "thankless child" (p. 77) to his parents. His father thinks that it is he who is responsible for his mother's deterioration. From his mother's view, he is an unwanted child. His mother says to him : "You were born afraid. Because I was so afraid to bring you into the world" (p. 96). Even his jealous brother, who is the cause of his misery, asks in a defensive manner : "Then who are you blaming? Edmund, for being born?" (p. 34). Perhaps, through the voice of Jamie, O'Neill wants to convey his philosophy of life. Man is born to suffer and nobody is particularly responsible for his doom. But in truth, it is the circumstances and his insight into life which force Edmund to lead a solitary life.

His father's stinginess, his mother's love-hate attitude, his brother's envious nature and, above all, his poetic nature are the combined forces behind his lonely suffering. He falls a prey to tuberculosis. His father, however, wants to send him to state-owned Sanatorium so that he may not spend much on his cure. Edmund blames his father, recalling the case of his mother. As he is more attached to his mother, he feels the load of his mother's dope-addiction, weighing heavy on his heart. Like his mother, he avoids reality and seeks an escape into the fog of unreality :

> The fog was where I wanted to be... Everything looked and sounded unreal... I wanted-to be alone with myself in another world where truth is untrue and life can hide from itself... I even lost the feeling of being on land... As if I was a ghost belonging to the fog, and the fog was the ghost of the sea. It felt damned peaceful to be nothing more than a ghost within a ghost (p. 113).

Like Mary, he never finds peace in the summer-house and remains a stranger to his family. Actually, the poet within him keeps him apart from others. He does not identify himself with them and loses his sense of belongingness. Therefore, he searches an identity of his own in a world beyond human reach. He expresses his longing for the vision of beauty in a dreamy state :

> It was a great mistake, my being born a man, I would have been much more successful as a sea-gull or a fish. As it is, I will always be a stranger, who never feels at home, who does not really want and is not really wanted, who can never belong.... (p. 135).

In this regard, Edmund Tyrone can be compared with Robert Mayo of *Beyond the Horizon*. Both the men are seekers of beauty; both are dissatisfied with the life provided to them and suffer from a sense of isolation. Unable to find any solution, Edmund hopes to find the lost sense of belonging in a state of unreality like Robert's quest of hope — what lies beyond the horizon. Edmund hopes to find it in his mystic oneness with the sea :

> I dissolved in the sea, became white sails and flying spray, became beauty and rhythm, became moonlight and the ship and the high dim-starred sky! I belonged, without past or future, within peace and unity and a wild joy, within something greater than my own life, or the life of Man, to

> Life itself. To God, if you want to put it that way (p. 134).

The theme of alienation is also projected through the title of the play and the symbols used in it. The title, *Long Day's Journey into Night*, is very suggestive. It signifies the characters' separation from reality. It is not a forward journey but a journey in the backward direction, especially for Mary. For her, it is a sad journey into the fog of dope and dream which clearly separates her from reality. For Jamie, it is a hopeless journey into the night of cynicism and frustration. For him, it begins and ends in darkness, offering him nothing to soothe his agitated mind. For James, it is a tragic journey down the wrong road, away from his earlier commercial triumph. And for Edmund, it is a journey beyond night in a hopeful state of unreality.

Like the title, the symbols are also suggestive and add much more to expose the theme. "Home" is the most important symbol that creates the deep sense of isolation in its inhabitants. Home is normally a place for man's physical and spiritual shelter, but in this play it ironically suggests loneliness and alienation. It is a home, but everyone feels homeless here. Although it is ironically called the "Summer house," but there is no sign of summer or sunshine in it. Mary never finds herself belonging to it. The symbol 'wedding gown' signifies her search for happiness that she has lost since her marriage. The symbols of 'fog' and 'foghorn' also convey the same meaning of isolation and separation. 'Fog' symbolizes the world of unreality that separates man from reality and makes him a stranger in the eyes of others. It is a potential symbol of man's ignorance about himself and his failure to understand others in this fog-ridden world. It also stands for oblivion and self-deception. The constant use of fog signifies the characters' escapes from a world of reality to a world of unreality.

The play is a woeful tale of isolation and loneliness. In it O'Neill has painted the most tragic picture of the shattered dreams in an autobiographical manner. All the four haunted Tyrones torment themselves and one another, gradually stripping away every protective illusion until each one faces himself and others without hope. The driving force among them forces each of the members into his own disintegration, and causes him to take others with him. Doris V. Falk rightly opines :

> All the Tyrones are doomed to destroy and be destroyed, to be victimized not only by each other but by the dead, for the dead have willed them a heritage of disease, alcoholism and drug addiction, and have cursed them with the deeper ills of alienation, conflict, and self-destructiveness.[10]

3. *A TOUCH OF THE POET* (1942)

A Touch of the Poet (1942) was published after the death of Eugene O'Neill. He had finished the writing of this play a decade before his death. Actually, he planned it for his proposed cycle of plays "The Tale of Possesser's Self-Dispossessed," but the cycle remained incomplete. Although he has written other few plays, but *A Touch of the Poet* is the only completed play of the cycle.[11] O'Neill intended the cycle to record the rise of an Irish family in America and its struggle to establish itself in conflict with the hostile and exploitative Yankees. Though this conflict provides the background for *A Touch of the Poet,* the play's real theme is the tragic suffering of a character from isolation and loneliness, which arise due to the conflict between his proud illusion and shameful reality.

The play depicts the story of Melody family, particularly of Cornelius Melody, who is unable to harmonize and reconcile the pride of his former glory with the shame of his present destitution. Con Melody, the aristocratically raised son of an Irish tavern-keeper, after passing a military career, becomes the owner of Melody's tavern. Snubbed by Yankee aristocrats and hated by the Irish because of his contempt for them, the handsome Melody lives in a dream-world where he is still the refined Major. He haughtily recites Byron before the mirror and rides his thorough-bred mare. This indulgence has improvised him and worn out his wife, Nora, whom he dislikes for her coarse Irish ways and looks. But she forgives and worships him, begs shopkeepers for credit, and does manual labour to support his illusion. Sara, the daughter in whom are combined his aristocratic and Nora's peasant characteristics, is torn between pride and bitter hatred of his father, and they fight each other viciously. On his annual celebration of the Battle of Talavera, in which Cornelius distinguished himself with Wellington, Sara swears that this is the last time she will play waitress to him and to his invited guests, and decides to marry Simon Harford, a Yankee capitalist's son now lying sick upstairs. Sara loves Simon for his poetic quality and dreamy nature.

Though undaunted by a warning visit from Simon's curiously neutral mother, Deboran, Sara fears that Melody's bungling interference will ruin her chances of happiness. When old Harford's lawyer appears with a cash offer to prevent his son's marriage to a lowly bar-keeper's daughter, Melody's stiff Irish pride sends him out into the night, determined to mend his wounded honor. In the privacy of Simon's bedroom, Sara elicits Simon's vow to marry her, after which Melody returns home, having brawled with the police and Harford's servant. Thoroughly mortified and disillusioned, Melody gives up his proud dream and ridicules his former pretensions of being Byronic. He reverts to his Irish brogue, and melodramatically shoots his beloved mare — the symbol of what used to be the aristocratic major. The result of Cornelius' broken dream leaves the family in a bitter state.

Man's rootlessness and his inability to find a sense of belonging leave him a state of isolation. This happens in the case of Con Melody, the protagonist of the play. His suffering from rootlessness starts from the beginning of his life, when his wealthy Irish father sends him to Dublin in order to make him a gentleman. Unfortunately, he is not accepted by his aristocratic schoolmates. As a result, his life becomes a constant rebellion against his humble Irish origin, on the one hand, and the snobbery of the gentry, on the other. Since then Con Melody tries to exist on his aristocratic pretensions, detesting the Irish scum, wherein he has his real roots. By rejecting his own origin, he rejects his own self and becomes alien to his true self. In this regard, his self-alienation can be compared with that of Brutus Jones of *The Emperor Jones*, who denies his negro origin by hating the negroes and becomes isolated from his own people. Like Jones, Con also faces the problem of identity that he has lost due to his false ego of aristocracy.

After leading a poor life of tavern-keeper, he also suffers from the same sense of isolation from self and society that he experienced in Europe. Micky Maloy, one of the associates of Con's tavern, says :

> The damned Yankee gentry won't let him come near them, and he considers the few Irish around here to be scum beneath his notice.[12]

The aristocratic Yankees do not accept him as one of their own, while to the Irish immigrants in America he becomes an alien, an outsider. Thus, he is unable to belong to anywhere. His falsity keeps him apart from both the societies. He knows that he is beyond the pail of the established Boston families, but his self-pretensions do not allow him to identify himself with the Irish immigrants and leave him in a state of illusion.

His approach towards life, based on feudalistic pretensions, makes him a Byronic hero, who recites from Byron's "Child Harold" in front of mirror and creates a false self-image for himself. Perhaps, through the character of Con Melody, O'Neill tries to recollect his past, as Arthur and Barbara Gelb remarks : "Like Cornelius Melody, the haughty, embittered, self-pitying hero of *A Touch of the Poet*, Eugene enjoyed quoting the lines from Byron's Child Harold...."[13] O'Neill describes his physical appearance and manner in which one can find the reflection of his age :

> It is his face that reveals the ravages of dissipation — a ruined face... There is a look of wrecked distinction about it, of brooding, humiliated pride. His manner is that of a polished gentleman. Too much so, he overdoes it and one soon feels that he is overplaying a role which has become more real than his real self to him (p. 27).

Con Melody avoids the present reality by immersing in his glorious past that separates him from the truth. In the midst of bankruptcy, he invites his old associates to mark the occasion of his old victory. He recollects :

> It's a far cry from this dunghill on which I rot to that glorious day when the Duke of Wellington — Lord Welsely, then — did me the honor before the army to commend my bravery (p. 30).

Though he realizes his own conditions, yet his ego does not permit him to make any compromise. When his wife suggests him to wear the Major's uniform, he says : "It makes me feel at least the ghost of the man I was then" (p. 31). The real Major in him is dead, but the ghost still lingers; and Melody is perpetually haunted by this invincible spectre. His separation from the present can be exemplified through his own words : "Faith, I was far away in spirit, lost in memories of a glorious battle in Spain, nineteen years ago, "today" (p. 45).

Melody's illusion not only keeps him apart from the present, but also forces him to lead an estranged life within his family. His false aristocratic ego causes a lot of trouble to his wife and daughter, who is never satisfied with him. She cannot bear her father's gentlemanly pretensions, particularly when they mean the family's starvation. When Sara learns that the payment of Dickenson's feed-bill for the mare has been preferred to the payment of the family's barest needs, she flares up in anger. She sneers at her father's aristocratic pretensions at the cost of the family's survival :

> The mare comes first, if she takes the bread out of our mouth. The grand gentleman must have his throughbred to ride out in state.... (p. 18).

Although his wife suffers a lot to keep his pipe-dream alive, still he does not like her. He considers that she is a woman below his status. But his daughter blames him for his indifferent attitude towards his wife. She says to her mother :

> I do hate him for the way he treats you. I heard him again last night, raking up the past, and blaming his ruin on his having to marry you (p. 20).

It clearly shows how he passes his life without any understanding with his daughter and wife. Turning between reality and illusion, Con Melody realizes the truth for a moment, but soon he denies the truth. He says to himself :

> Driven from pillar to post in my own home. Everywhere ignorance — or the scorn of my own daughter. (*Then defiantly*) But by the Eternal God, no power on earth, nor in hell itself, can break me.... (p. 51).

The duality in his character is the main cause of his isolation. In this respect, he reminds us of James Tyrone of *Long Day's Journey into Night*. Melody lives with the memory of a great honor — *viz.*, Willington's praise after Talavera — just as Tyrone recalls Booth's praise of his acting. Both have a touch of the peasant as well as the poet in them. Both reject modernity — Melody by hating Jacksonian democracy, and Tyrone by denying modern authors. Due to this duality, both are alienated from their wives and children.

Con Melody's concept of gentleman shatters when he rushes to the Harford's home to avenge his pride. Being beaten by the police and humiliated by Harford, he finally returns to his own self. He feels, he is no longer the major but the son of the Irish shebeen-keeper. He kills the mare which is the symbol of his false aristocracy. His pipe-dream vanishes when he comes face to face with his illusion. His killing of mare can be compared with Hickey's self-surrender; both commit spiritual suicide when they find they can no longer believe in their pipe-dreams. Though by shooting the mare he shoots his illusion, yet the realization comes after a lot of suffering from isolation and separation.

Nora Melody, the innocent wife of Con, suffers from the same sense of isolation throughout her life. She is a victim of her husband's indifferent attitude. Her husband dislikes her and hates her, for her Irish peasantry origin. From the day of her marriage Con never provides a happy life to her. Her husband considers the marriage as a forced act by the priest. For this reason, Con hates the priest. He also hates Nora because she has a constant faith in the priest. After her marriage, Con joins army, leaving the pregnant Nora to lead a lonely life. So, Nora is deprived of her husband's love just after her marriage. Jamie Cregan describes her tragic suffering of separation as follows :

> He married her because he'd fallen in love with her, but he was ashamed of her in his pride at the same time because her folks were only ignorant peasants on his estate, as poor as poor... he married her and then went off to the war, and left her alone in the castle to have her child, and never saw her again till he was sent home from Spain (p. 12).

Even after returning from the Army when Con prefers to lead his life in falsity, she remains a stranger to him. Even in the most intimate moment of their relation, Con never hesitates to accuse her : "Why don't you wash your hair? It turns my stomach with its stink of onions and stew" (p. 33). But he forgets that he is the person who reduces her life to a housemaid. Although the Irish peasant in Con loves her in his way, but the Major despises her. He does not allow her interference in any of his matters. Throughout her life, she remains an alien wife due to her husband's false ego. She pathetically utters : "Has he ever cared for anyone except himself and his pride?" (p. 105).

Ironically, Nora is the only person who keeps Con's pipe-dream alive and becomes the worst sufferer for it. Instead of his constant nagging, she always loves her husband and remains loyal to him at the cost of her happiness. Her daughter bitterly comments on her mother's loyalty which is the real cause of her suffering. She says : "You bear all his insults as meek as a lamb; You keep on slaving for him when it's that has made you old before your time" (p. 20). But, in defence, Nora replies : "There's no slavery in it when you love!" (p. 21). To her, true love means total surrender which is the only pride for a wife; she helplessly requests her daughter not to take away that pride from her. Without that, her life is nothing, but a meaningless existence. This is the reality behind her constant submission and forgiveness to her husband. In this regard, she reminds us of Evelyn, the alien wife of Hickey of *The Iceman Cometh*. Like Evelyn, Nora forgives her husband and tries to get happiness through illusion. Both the wives fail to get any real happiness, and remain alienated from their husbands.

Sara's suffering is something different from that of her mother. Nora suffers because of her excessive-love to her husband, and Sara's dissatisfaction emanates from her hatred for her father. Both the daughter and the mother reveal their respective brands of pride. Sara is proud of her freedom, while Nora is proud of her bondage. Sara is downright earthy and pragmatic in her attitude to her father and the world in general; Nora is reverential and idealistic in her attitude towards her husband. Sara is impatient with her father, but Nora is the very image of monumental patience. Sara suffers along with her mother and is separated from her father physically from the beginning of her childhood. Even when she starts living with her father, she is separated from him mentally. Her relation with her father is somewhat parallel to the relation between James Tyrone and Jamie of *Long Day's Journey into Night*. Jamie hates his father for his stinginess; but in the case of Sara, she hates her father for his false aristocracy.

Sara does not share her father's self-delusion in thinking of himself as a gentleman. She becomes disgusted with the life provided to her. She says bitterly :

> I've had need to have, to hold my head up slaving as a waitress and chambermaid so my father can get drunk every night like a gentleman.... (p. 26).

There is a fierce antagonism throughout between Sara and Con Melody. She resents his treatment of her mother; she is continually reminding him that they are poor because of his extravagance and his capacity in business. He oscillates between treating her as a servant, and behaving with an elaborate chill courtesy. Through the mare she attacks her father's falsity because of his inhuman preference for an animal over the human needs of the family. Out of disgust, she says to her father :

> If you ever dared face the truth, you'd hate and despise yourself : (*Passionately*) All I pray to God is that some day when you're admiring yourself in the mirror something will make you see at last what you really are. That will be revenge in full for all you've done to Mother and me.... (p. 80).

Although Sara hates her father's illusion and dislikes her mother's total surrender, yet she is the real combination of both the qualities. As O'Neill describes her : "There is a curious blending in her of what are commonly considered aristocratic and peasant characteristics" (p. 13). Perhaps this is the reason why she becomes a split personality. She represents both her father's false aristocracy and her mother's instincts for selfless love. Her mother's loyalty forces her to love Simon Harford and her father's false pride compels her to dream a wealthy life through marriage. In order to fulfil her dream, she loves Simon, but does not want to be a slave like her mother. Motivated by love and ambition, she allows Simon to seduce her. Her act of seduction is the cause of her insecurity. Surrendering herself physically to Simon, she is confident to reach close to her dreams.

After her surrender to Simon, she gradually becomes like her mother. The aristocratic ego, which she has inherited from her father, begins to crumble. She finds : "...whatever meant happiness to him (Simon) would be my only ambition" (p. 111). In this context, she reminds us of Abbie Putnam of *Desire Under the Elms*, who traps herself in the efforts of trapping Eben Cabot. Sara's dream shatters with final realization; she says to her mother :

> Isn't that a joke on me, with all my crazy dreams of riches and a grand estate and me a haughty lady riding around, in a carriage with Coachman and footman.... (p. 111).

Although the play does not reveal what happens to this alien daughter of Melody after her marriage to Simon Harford, but from her attitude towards life, one can imagine that she may not be able to get any satisfaction from her poetic-natured husband.

The theme of isolation is also projected through the character of Simon Harford, who never appears in the play. So far the stage is concerned, he remains as a shadow figure throughout. We come to know about his isolated life through the discussion of other characters of the play. He is the son of a rich Yankee tradesman, Henery Harford. He "has a touch of the poet in him" (p. 24) that keeps him apart from others. Being separated from his wealthy parents, he leads an isolated life in the tavern of Melody. Like his predecessors, Robert Mayo of *Beyond the Horizon* and Dion Anthony of *The Great God Brown*, he is a dreamer and a worshipper of nature. He imagines himself as a poet and a hermit, and this is the real cause behind his estrangement. O'Neill describes the dreams of his ideal hero through Sara :

> He wanted to prove his independence by living alone in the wilds, and build his own cabin, and do all the work, and support himself simply and feel one with Nature, and think great thoughts about what life means, and write a book about how the world can be changed so people won't be greedy to own money and land and get the best of each other but will be content with little and live in peace and freedom together, and it will be like heaven on earth (pp. 23-4).

These are dreams only because he fails to write the book. Instead of writing the Utopia, he writes love poems and falls in love with Sara. When a person fails in his attempt, he becomes more limited, finite, depersonalized and thus fragmented and alienated in his limited sphere of existence than ever before. He becomes an object, an isolated thing, which is subjected to diverse forces that externally influence him as a magnetic object. So Simon's acceptance of Sara is probably the result of that diversion and his long suffering due to isolation. But will he be able to get rid of that after marrying her? This is the question that O'Neill leaves for his audience.

Another character, who is a victim of alienation, is Deborah Harford, the mother of Simon. She has a brief appearance in the play. She comes to the tavern to meet her alien son. Her discussions with Sara reveal the tragic story of her isolated life. She is a withdrawn figure, confined to her house, garden and books. She is alienated from her husband and isolated from the family. She hates the tyrannic attitude of Harfords.

She tells Sara : "You can have no idea what revengefull hate the Harford pursuit of freedom imposed upon the women who shared their lives" (p. 64). While exposing the characteristics of Harfords, she warns Sara; but at the same time it reveals her own desperation and isolation from life particularly from her husband.

The title and the setting evoke the same sense of detachment. The title, *A Touch of the Poet*, expresses the isolation of the characters, especially of Con Melody and Simon Harford. Both the characters have the same poetic touch in them, and this is cause of their sufferings. One is middle-aged, backward-looking, selfish, often cruel; while the other is young, idealistic, forward-looking, aspiring to be a poet and philosopher. Both the men are alienated from their immediate present. Similarly, the description of Melody's tavern with its deteriorated condition symbolizes the ruined life of Con Melody. He says : "This inn, like myself, has fallen upon unlucky days" (p. 53). The different sections of the house give a visual equivalent to the inner division of Melody. To some extent, the bar and the dining-room with its drunken associates serve the purpose of Harry Hope's Saloon. For Con, the bar-room and its associates provide an escape. The bar is the only place where he can merge with his dreams without any fear of contradiction.

4. *A MOON FOR THE MISBEGOTTON* (1953)

A Moon for the Misbegotton is the last completed play by O'Neill. In this play, O'Neill tells the tragic story of his elder brother, Jamie O'Neill, through the character of James Tyrone Jr., one of the doomed protagonists of the play. Through him the dramatist demonstrates man's quest for identity in a world of nothingness and emptiness, marked by the insurmountable barriers of human communication, the perpetual tension between illusion and reality, man's cosmic loneliness, the haunting reality of man's past, and the eternal conflict between life and death. About this play, Arthur and Barbara Gelb opines :

> ...the play is among O'Neill's greatest, rich in Irish humor and enormously moving in its brutal tragedy — a powerful expression of individualism for a dramatist who wrote to the sound of strange harmonies within his own soul and his disregard for the conventions of Broadway.[14]

The play is a sequel to *Long Day's Journey into Night*, and it begins eleven years after the end of the previous play. As in *Long Day's Journey into Night*, in this play the playwright uses a single setting, and the physical action of the play takes place during a single day that journeys through a moonlit night to a new strange dawn.

The play opens in Connecticut at the house of the tenant farmer Phil Hogan on a day in early September. Phil Hogan, the shrewd, garrulous farmer lives with his daughter and younger son. When the play begins, his son Mike is about to leave the home and his father. Like his two elder brothers, he wants to sever from his father because of his rude and indifferent attitude towards them. Josie, his over-sized daughter, a virgin with the habit of pretending promiscuity, lives in a state of illusion. She hates her father and loves Tyrone, their drunken landlord. Mike, knowing that Josie love Tyrone, tells her that the latter has planned to sell the farm to Harder, their hostile neighbor. This is false, but Mike thinks that it may help to bring Josie and Tyrone together. Keeping the view of his parted son, Hogan plans to play the trick to protect their tenancy. He suggests her that she should persuade Tyrone to sleep with her and then they can force him to marry her. Josie, enraged by Tyrone's apparent indifference, agrees to the plan. But James, in a drunken mood, rejects her advances because he truly loves her, reassuring her that the farm will not be sold.

When Tyrone comes to visit her in night, she learns more about his state of mind and his lonely suffering due to isolation. The moonlit-night reveals the dark aspects of both the characters. Tyrone confesses his inconsolable grief over his mother's death, and his remorse at his degenerate behavior on the train while bringing the body back from California. Realizing the unutterable sadness of Tyrone's life, Josie says goodbye and prays that he may soon find deliverance in the death he longs for, and that he may rest for ever in forgiveness and peace. With the diminishing of moonlit-night, the misbegotten lovers are separated from each other for the rest of their lives.

This powerful drama, which O'Neill wrote in the memory of his brother, mainly deals with the tragic suffering of three isolated persons. They are Phil Hogan, Josie and James Tyrone Jr., who represents O'Neill's brother, Jamie. All these characters suffer from a sense of alienation, and lead an estranged life.

Phil Hogan, the greedy farmer, suffers from inter-family alienation. His coarseness and rough manner keep him apart from his sons and daughter. His two elder sons, Thomas and John, have already left him before the play's beginning. Now, his younger son plans to leave him. His love for money and possessiveness reminds us of Ephraim Cabot of *Desire Under the Elms.* Like the Old Cabot, Phil Hogan also believes in the hard work which is the main cause of his estrangement within his family. He treats them like slaves. As Josie says to her brother Hike :

> You cant't stand up to the Old Man, any more than Thomas or John could, and the old devil would always keep you a slave.[15]

His materialistic attitude makes him a stranger even in his family. When he comes to know that Josie has stolen his money and helped Mike, he accuses her : "A fine curse God put on me when he gave me a daughter as big and strong as a bull, and as vicious and disrespectful" (p. 24). Expressing his hatred towards his sons, he admits : "To tell the truth, I never liked him.... And I never liked Thomas and John, either" (p. 25). Being dissatisfied with his children, he pathetically recollects his dead wife who was the only person to understand him. He tells that after the death of his wife, he has lost his faith in God. He says : "I've never set foot in a church since and never will" (p. 26). It clearly indicates that Hogan is separated not only from his family but also from God. His tragic alienation from his daughter is evident when he says :

> I never thought I'd see the day when a daughter of mine would be such a coward as to threaten her old father when he's helpless drunk and can't hit back (p. 73).

Although Hogan blames his daughter and scolds her like anything else, yet at the same time he is worried about her future. His plan of trapping Tyrone through her, is the main reason of it. Undoubtedly, he partly gets success in his scheme by possessing the farm, but he is not able to provide her a secure life. After the departure of Tyrone, he reveals to her daughter :

> I wanted you to find happiness — by hook or crook, one way or another, what did I care now? ...And if I gave a thought to his money at all, that was the least of it, and why shouldn't I want to have you live in ease and comfort for a change, like you deserve, instead of in this shanty on a lously farm, slaving for me? (p. 154).

His estrangement is the cause of his love-hate relationship with his daughter. It is like that of James Tyrone Sr., of *Long Day's Journey into Night* and Con Melody of *A Touch of the Poet*. Like them, Phil Hogan also suffers from isolation and separation.

Josie, the only female character of the play, is also a victim of isolation. Death has separated her from her mother and from her childhood. In place of a loving father, she finds a money-loving farmer, for whom, she is nothing but a maid servant. In this context, she can be compared with Sara

Melody, the alien daughter of Con Melody of *A Touch of the Poet*. All her three brothers have left her one by one, leaving her to suffer with her greedy father. So, leading an isolated life, she becomes more violent and loses the softness of a woman. O'Neill describes her in these words :

> She is so oversize for a woman that she is almost a freak.... She is more powerful than any, but an exceptionally strong man, able to do the manual labour of two ordinary men. But there is no manish quality about her. She is all woman (p. 13).

She is, thus, a woman divided against herself; her physical appearance is at variance with her inner being. Though born an unusual girl, she longs to be a simple, unpretentious and ordinary in every way. But she fails to achieve that. Her pretension of promiscuity is the result of that failure and bitter experience in life. The mask of the whore, through which she hides the reality makes her a split person. It is like a pipe-dream, through which she wants to mitigate the pain of isolation in a state of illusion. But her dream shatters when she meets Tyrone. Her pride that she is a slut begins to crumble with the interference of Tyrone, who pleads :

> You can take the truth, Josie — from me. Because you and I belong to the same club. We can kid the world but we can't fool ourselves, like most people, no matter what we do — nor escape ourselves, no matter where we run away... We'd find our own ghosts there waiting to greet us.... (p. 121).

It is not a simple suggestion from Tyrone to Josie for facing the truth. Rather, it is the message of the playwright, who wants to convey the ultimate truth of human life that a man cannot escape from the bitter realities of life without facing them. When she refuses to admit the truth, Tyrone replies : "Pride is the sin by which the angels fell. Are you going to keep that up-with me?" (p. 121).

Josie's acceptance of Tyrone's love is the result of her shattered illusion. When she fails to suppress and call of her inner being, she falls in love with him. It is a kind of love that arises out of the intensely human need of two persons to communicate with each other, and to understand their relationship with life itself. But their love defies all categorization in terms of a definite social relationship. With their final realization, they feel that they would fulfil each other's need. But, ultimately, it is only Tyrone who is able to fulfil his need. As Travis Bogard says : "...whatever, there is of tribute in Jamie's love creates for, her, a solace, not unlike that, which she brings to him."[16] As for Josie, her desire is doomed to failure, for she cannot love a man who is already dead. She tries to reveal the nature of her tragic fate when she tells her father in the morning that she is like a "Virgin who bears a dead child in the night, and the drawn finds her still a virgin" (pp. 140-141). In spite of all the difficulties and dissatisfactions, she must live to face the problems of life through the haze of sadness and frustration that hangs over her.

The most important figure, the fated hero of the play, James Tyrone, is the tragic victim of isolation and loneliness. He is haunted by the feeling of guilt that he committed at the time of his mother's death. After her death, he becomes more helpless and insecure. Early in the play, the characters drop hints about Tyrone being a dead and doomed person. Phil Hogan says about him : "He'll suddenly turn strange, and look sad, and stare at nothing as if he was mourning over some ghost inside him" (p. 39). But Josie's description of him, when she compares him to "a dead man walking slow behind his own coffin" (p. 41), is more telling. The fact that Tyrone is no more than a corpse is brought out when Josie, after kissing him, says, "It's like kissing a corpse" (p. 54).

He is a lonely man, haunted by his own ghosts, trying desperately to exorcise them. But the shadows of his past will not let him breathe in freedom. For him, there is no hope but oblivion. He is probably the least dramatic of any of O'Neill's protagonists; his role in the play is a long self-analysis, an endless case history of self-hatred and alienation. He, like Jamie in *Long Day's Journey into Night*, wears two masks. O'Neill describes him as follows :

> ...his face a certain Mephistophelean quality which accentuated by his habitually cynical experession. But when he smiles without sneering, he still has the ghost of a former youthful irresponsible Irish charm — that of the beguiling ne'er-do-well, sentimental and romantic (p. 42).

With this duality, when he talks about his tragic suffering to Josie, he alternates between his two selves. Expansive at one moment, submissive at another, he does not know his real identity and withdraws from both the selves. One mask reveals his disintegration with the self, and another exposes his self-hatred. Oscillating between both the masks, he becomes an alien to his present reality. He himself admits : "There is no present or future — only the past happening over and over again — now. You can't get away from it" (pp. 115-16).

Tyrone himself accepts the fact that he has been virtually dead since his mother died. He expresses his guilt to Josie in terms of his life-long hatred of his father, love, and guilty, longing for his mother. About his relationship with his father, he speaks to Josie : "...I hated him, anyway — as much as he hated me" (p. 116). After the death of his father, he stopped drinking for the sake of his mother because she did not like it at all. But when she became ill, James again started drinking. To his ill-luck, his mother discovered it before her death, and this filled him with a sense of guilt. James tries to forget the incident, but he always fails in his attempt. He expresses his tragic agony by remembering his mother at the time of her death in those words :

> But there are things I can never forget — the undertakers, and her body in a coffin with her

> face made up. I couldn't hardly recognize her... practically a stranger. To whom I was a stranger. Cold and indifferent. Not worried about any more. Free at last. Free from worry. From pain. From me (p. 131).

For James, this is the beginning of his misery. The final realization comes after his physical involvement with the whore in the train while carrying the body of his mother. After this incident, he is tortured by a sense of guilt constantly. He never finds any peace. Life becomes meaningless to him.

Tyrone's passionate attachment with Josie under the moonlit night is nothing but the result of his love for his mother. Although, for a night he is able to achieve his lost mother's love through Josie, but he realizes that it is almost impossible to achieve it permanently. It is the fulfilment of his desire of lost mother's love in a state of illusion, which is never possible in reality. So, he must leave Josie, and must live to face the bitter consequences of the life in a state of solitude.

The theme of isolation and loneliness is well projected through the dramatic technique used by O'Neill. Like almost all his other plays, the setting of the play is both realistic and symbolic. The action of the play takes place in a farmhouse. The playwright describes it thus :

> The House is not, to speak mildly, a fine example of New England architecture, placed so perfectly in its setting that it appears a harmonious part of the landscape, rooted in the earth. It has been moved to its present site, and looks it (p. 11).

The house is symbolic of man's desolation and alienation from nature. The central conflict in James — between his youthful, irresponsible charm and his middle-aged self-destructiveness — is paralleled by the tension in the contrasting element of the setting. The window panes of the house are missing. The setting, on the whole, is an image of Tyrone's helplessness and is withdrawal from the mainstream of life. Another significant part of the setting is provided by a big boulder with a flat-top, close to the house under the window next to Josie's bedroom. The boulder is a complex symbol, suggesting many different things. On the one hand, it is a symbol of Josie, on the other, it suggests the hard life of Hogans. Like the boulder, Josie is destined to stay in the farm house, separated from the outer world that lies beyond the house.

Like its setting, the title, *A Moon for the Misbegotten*, is also aptly suggestive. So far as the word 'misbegotten' is concerned, it refers to the person at the bottom of the society and can rightly be applicable to Josie and James. Their conditions clearly convey that they are no or better than the misbegotton. The moon, throwing its soft light over the two misbegotton creatures, symbolizes the world of human values, of understanding, pity, love and forgiveness, required to save life from utter despair and emptiness. In spite of all the glooms and frustrations that surround them, they find a glimpse of meaning in their strange love and understanding of each other. But the irony is that the moon, which has united the misbegotton lovers, separates them with its disappearance.

REFERENCES

[1] Doris V. Falk, *Eugene O'Neill and the Tragic Tension*, p. 157.

[2] *Selected Letters of Eugene O'Neill*, ed. Travis Bogard and Jackson R. Bryer, p. 511.

[3] Rosamond Gilder, "The Iceman Cometh", *O'Neill and His Plays*, ed. Oscar Cargil, *et al.*, p. 203.

[4] *Selected Plays of Eugene O'Neill*, p. 631. Hereafter the quotes from *The Iceman Cometh* will refer to this edition and be indicated only by the page number in parenthesis in the body of this study.

[5] Brooks Atkinson, "The Iceman Cometh," *O'Neill and His Plays*, ed. Oscar Cargil, *et al.*, p. 213.

[6] Doris V. Falk, *Eugene O'Neill and the Tragic Tension*, p. 162.

[7] E.A. Engel, *The Haunted Heroes of Eugene O'Neill* (Cambridge : Harvard Univ. Press, 1953), p. 286.

[8] O'Neill, *Long Day's Journey into Night* (London : Janathan Cape, 1962), p. 58. Hereafter, the quotes from *Long Day's Journey into Night* will refer to this edition and be indicated only by the page number in parenthesis in the body of this study.

[9] Travis Bogard, *Contour in Time*, p. 433.

[10] Doris V. Falk, *Eugene O'Neill and the Tragic Tension*, p. 182.

[11] Arthur and Barbara Gelb, *O'Neill*, p. 847.

[12] O'Neill, *A Touch of the Poet* (London : Jonathan Cape, 1957), p. 11. Hereafter, the quotes from *A Touch of the Poet* will refer to this edition and be indicated only by the page number in parenthesis in the body of this study.

[13] Arthur and Barbara Gelb, *O'Neill*, p. 147.

[14] Arthur and Barbara Gelb, *O'Neill*, p. 849.

[15] O'Neill, *A Moon for the Misbegotten* (London : Janathan Cape, 1960), p. 17. Hereafter, the quotes from *A Moon for the Misbegotten* will refer to this edition and be indicated only by the page number in the parenthesis in the body of this study.

[16] Travis Bogard, *Contøur in Times*, p. 450.

5

Conclusion

An examination of Eugene O'Neill's plays in the foregone chapters leads us to certain conclusions regarding the theme of isolation and loneliness explored through an analysis of their plots, situations, characters, dialogues and techniques. It may be affirmed that O'Neill is mainly concerned with the sociological, cultural and personal isolation of the individuals who are estranged from one another, and communication and mutual understanding in their lives are replaced by estrangement and hostility. His plays reveal the social life where one individual looks upon the other as a hostile force. There comes a state when he becomes isolated and estranged not only from others but also from himself.

O'Neill, being an existentialist, deals with life in a very realistic and authentic manner, and presents a faithful dramatization of human situation. The most important issue of the contemporary American society is man's failure to "belong" or to find roots anywhere in this hostile world. Man is isolated not only from himself but also from nature, culture, society, religion and God. He is a lost and lonely soul, and suffers from a sense of anguish as is already evinced through the alienation of Robert Mayo in *Beyond the Horizon*, Jones in *The Emperor Jones*, Yank in *The Hairy Ape*, Jim Harris and Ella in *All God's Chillun Got Wings* as well as the protagonists in the other plays under this study. This sense of isolation and loneliness of the characters in his plays arises out of the American socio-cultural and spiritual milieu. Man's desire to belong is shown in *Mourning Becomes Electra*, and in it we find the utter lack of any sustaining faith in the present time.

The sense of isolation and loneliness in the plays of O'Neill causes suffering to his characters, and their failure to control it in an effective manner brings tragedy in their lives. This isolation and loneliness may originate from a painful sense of separation from those with whom one has a striking intellectual or spiritual affinity. It looks ironical when one feels a total stranger in the very place where he intensely wants to live with a sense of belongingness. An isolated person in his plays is one whom circumstances have forced into a self-recognition of separatedness, resulting in his suffering. *The Iceman Cometh* shows how man's inability to cope with life can create a feeling of isolation and loneliness in his life, forcing him to withdraw from others. The play effectively dramatizes the alienation and sufferings of the inhabitants of Harry Hope's Saloon who have long broken their links with outside world and are living in a world of their own making. *The Great God Brown* shows how a man's persistent efforts to belong to Nature are thwarted by materialism, Christian asceticism, and socially-caused conflict in psyche. In *Mourning Becomes Electra*, the effect of the sense of isolation and loneliness is actually felt by all the members of the Mannon's family, and they are forced to bear its brunt.

We find that too much mechanization of modern life is also one of the important factors responsible to generate the sense of isolation, loneliness, estrangement and insecurity in the life of an individual. It has de-stabilized human life. *The Hairy Ape* shows how Yank is brutalized by an impersonal mechanical social order. Yank, in this play, is one who challenges the supremacy of the machine-age and sacrifices his life to move the workers by making them realize the necessity of revolt against their powerful masters. Besides the impersonal and mechanical social order, another factor responsible for the feeling of isolation and loneliness in O'Neill's heroes is their failure to discriminate between the world of dream and that of reality. His characters are the willing victims of romantic dreams or illusions; they suffer and feel isolated because of their refusal to give up their dreams. In *Beyond the Horizon*, Robert's romantic dream of going beyond the horizon is pushed beyond his pragmatic bent of mind. *The Iceman Cometh* also indicates how the destructive power of the romantic ideal stands in the way of man's forming a meaningful relationships with the real world, and how, finally, it is the cause of isolation and loneliness in his life. The same is true of the life of Dion Anthony of *The Great God Brown* and Simon Harford of *A Touch of the Poet*. Having failed in their search for romantic ideal, both of them are isolated from reality. In *Long Day's Journey into Night*, Edmund Tyrone's quest for beauty in a world of dreams is the principal cause of his estranged life.

Thus, in O'Neill's plays man's over-reaching craving for possessiveness and material gains is one of the vital causes of his isolation and loneliness. How the commercial civilization has made man spiritually bankrupt is given its finest expression through the characters of Ephraim Cabot in *Desire Under the Elms* and Billy Brown in *The Great God Brown*. Ephraim Cabot suffers from a sense of isolation due to his excessive materialistic attitude. His thirst for money keeps him apart and separated from his sons and wives. Similarly, Billy Brown exemplifies the successful but empty life of the materialist. He is inwardly empty and devoted only to the exterior things of life. *The Great God Brown* shows the isolation deeply rooted in American culture. It exposes those who seek money at the cost of truth and beauty, and remain severed from others and also from themselves. O'Neill always considers the acquisitive man as the root-cause of all the modern maladies. His is a voice against the craze of material success. To him, a money-minded person is quite complacement and steeped only in material values which cause his personal isolation and suffering. The isolation of James Tyrone and Phil Hogan from their families in *Long Day's Journey into Night* and in *A Moon for the Misbegotten*, respectively, is the cause of their excessive materialistic attitude.

O'Neill's characters suffer from isolation and loneliness also when they try to possess any human being by playing nasty tricks. This kind of possessiveness arises out of insecurity, and becomes the cause of their isolation. This forces Prof. Leeds of *Strange Interlude* to remain isolated from his daughter, Nina, when he tries to keep her as a possession for his security. Lavinia Mannon of *Mourning Becomes Electra* faces the same problem when she tries to possess her brother, Orin, for her security. Another character who becomes a victim of loneliness and isolation owing to this kind of possessiveness is Nina Leeds of *Strange Interlude*. She turns to be an alienated figure when she tries to possess all her desired men.

In the way of possessing others, the possessor sometimes becomes a possession and remains isolated for ever. The case in point is the tragic suffering and isolation of Abbie in *Desire Under the Elms* who tries to trap and possess Eben for the sake of her materialistic fulfilment, but becomes herself a possession of Eben. The suffering of Josie Hogan in *A Moon for the Misbegotten* is something parallel to that of Abbie. She is trapped by Jamie's selfless love when she tries to possess him, and finally remains isolated from him. Similarly, in *Strange Interlude*, Ned Darrell is forced to lead an isolated and lonely life of suffering when separated from his beloved and son after being trapped by the power of love. Also, it happens in the case of Christine Mannon and Adam Brant in *Mourning Becomes Electra*. Both the characters are trapped in the course possessing others, and remain isolated and lonely to face their doom. The possessiveness in Brant arises out of revenge, and Christine's is the result of her insecurity. But both are the victims of isolation and loneliness.

People in O'Neill's plays suffer from isolation and loneliness also owing to their false pride and ego. In *A Touch of the Poet*, Con Melody's false aristocracy is the source of his tragic suffering and isolation. He lives entirely in his memories of earlier gallantry in love and war. He always considers himself as the Major Cornelius Melody. In his pretensions of aristocracy, he hates his low-born wife and worships a high-bred mare, and thus remains lonely and isolated from the realities of life. In *Desire Under the Elms,* Ephraim's egotistical nature stands on his way, and his failure to adjust himself to new situations always plunges him into ever-increasing loneliness.

Another significant cause of man's isolation and loneliness is the search for the lost mother's love. It is an important aspect of O'Neill's plays. There is a profound love of a man for the lost mother, and it is symbol of lost happiness. Having failed to attain it, man remains isolated throughout his life. In The *Great God Brown,* Dion cries to be buried with his mother; and in *Desire Under the Elms*, Eben fails to forget his dead mother, who has been haunting his subconscious mind since the day of her death. In *Strange Interlude*, Charles Marsden suffers from isolation after the death of his mother. The suffering of Orin Mannon in *Mourning Becomes Electra* and Jamie in *A Moon for the Misbegotten* is the result of the search for lost mother's love. These characters suffer from isolation and loneliness after losing the love of their mothers. But in the case of Don Parritt of *The Iceman Cometh*, the search is something different. In it, O'Neill is preoccupied with the dual aspect of the 'mother-archetype' — both the giver and the destroyer of life. Orin tries to regain it through Lavinia. Jamie desperately wants to get in the arms of Josie, and Dion helplessly seeks it through Cybel, but none of them are able to recover it completely. Thus, they are forced to lead an estranged life, devoid of the love of a mother.

We find the sufferings of an individual in the plays of O'Neill through his isolation from 'self.' The characters in his plays are isolated and feel lonely due to their false pretensions and racial complex. In *A Touch of the Poet*, Con Melody is alienated from his self after rejecting his own Irish Origin. Jones in *The Emperor Jones* is a victim of self-alienation by hating the negroes to whom he really belongs. The characters in *Long Day's Journey into Night* also suffer from self-alienation. Each of them is lost and is in struggle with himself. Marry is isolated from self and is engaged in her past. Jamie's struggle is with himself. He has punished himself by taking wine and indulging in sex. Edmund's self-alienation is the result of his romantic outlook, his desire to identify with Nature.

Isolation in the plays of Eugene O'Neill is shown through the love-hate relationship among the characters. We find it in the case of Evelyn and Hickey in *The Iceman Cometh*. It again happens in the case of Nora and Con in *A Touch of The Poet*. Both the wives are isolated from their husbands owing to this type of relationship. It occurs not only between wife and husband, we witness it also in father-son, mother-son, and father-daughter relationships. In *Long Day's Journey into Night* James Tyrone's love-hate relationship with his sons is the cause of his estrangement. We observe that the same relationship exists between Mary and Jamie, and between Edmund and Jamie. In *A Moon for the Misbegotten*, both Josie and Phil are the victims of isolation and loneliness due to the love-hate relationship.

In O'Neill's opinion, man is a lonely sufferer in this helpless world. He finds himself totally isolated in a spiritually sterile universe and, therefore, cannot have a sense of harmony in it. In his search for identity, and also his need to belong, he feels his lostness more intensely. All the protagonists of his plays feel isolated, alienated, and despaired for lack of the centre of belonging. The tension in his plays is commonly related with the struggle against isolation and loneliness. We learn from his works that a man has to face tough times in a world without God, love and faith in life, and that he may belong, but it is possible only after sacrificing his life. It happens in the case of Yank, Robert Mayo and Orin Mannon.

Finally, this study reveals that the theme of isolation and loneliness is one of the variations on a common theme in American drama, *i.e.*, the theme of 'Quest' to which all the major playwrights are engaged in some form or the other. In the plays of Eugene O'Neill, however, this theme has been raised almost to a 'cult', a 'force' in human affairs that seems to dominate all the other aspects of life. Almost every one of the major characters displays a dream or a craving for the ideal that is outside his actual life. In most cases, the revealed situation is ironical. Fate and circumstances always so conspire against the dreamer that the dream not only becomes impossible but also a source of suffering and tragedy.

The work characteristically evinces that the treatment of isolation and loneliness in O'Neill's plays changes from the early to the later plays when his own outlook on life grows more pessimistic and negative. In the early plays, isolation and loneliness are caused by the vague and romantic dreams of the characters, who finally meet with the failure of unfulfilment of these dreams. In the later plays, O'Neill deals with that aspect of the dream of his characters which, with its rare flashes of revelation, keeps the dream alive and worth-pursuing. The character experiences a submerging of self into the universal whole in a mystical fashion. The character for a moment has a saint's vision of beatitude, as Edmund says in *Long Day's Journey into Night* : "For a second there is meaning! Then the hand lets the veil fall and you are alone, lost in the fog again, and you stumble on towards nowhere." This is the kind of 'isolation' we find in the later phase of O'Neill's literary career. We see here that isolation and loneliness make man spiritually shattered, and not only physically as in the early plays. Here, man feels isolated and lonely because his life is split between the dark reality and his sick existence on the one hand, and the eternal beauty of a permanent dream of mystical kind on the other. The dream merges into a mystical-spiritual experience and reveals the larger mystery of the universe itself. O'Neill comes to the realization that the quest for illusion or dream is meaningless and that only a recognition of the eternal unity manifest in God can bring comfort to the isolated, lonely and split soul of man.

O'Neill's plays of the three different phases show that his early plays deal with isolation and loneliness brought out through the failure of the romantic dreams, the dreams of escape. In the plays of the middle phase, isolation and loneliness is caused by the ugliness of reality for which he chooses the American social scene. In the later phase, isolation and loneliness are caused by the defeat or failure of the ideals, illusion and romantic dreams in actual life.

The tensions in O'Neill's plays are nearly always connected with man's struggle against isolation and loneliness. The secret of his dramatic intensity is to be found not in his theatricality, but in his rebellion and anger, and in his inability to resign himself to an arid view and way of life. He could not be at ease in a world without God, love and trust in life. His plays make it certain that he is the dramatist of failure, estrangement and isolation all through his illustrious literary career.

Select Bibliography

I. PRIMARY SOURCES

Dramatic Works of Eugene O'Neill

O'Neill, Eugene. *A Moon for the Misbegotten*. London : Jonathan Cape, 1960.

——. *A Touch of the Poet*. London : Jonathan Cape, 1957.

——. *Beyond the Horizon and Marco Millions*. London : Jonathan Cape Ltd., 1960.

——. *The Great God Brown and Lazarus Laughed*. London : Jonathan Cape, 1960.

——. *Long Day's Journey into Night*. London : Jonathan Cape, 1962.

——. *Nine Plays by O'Neill*. New York : Modern Library, 1941.

——. *The Plays of Eugene O'Neill*. New York : Random House, 1955.

——. *Selected Plays of Eugene O'Neill*. New York : Random House, 1967.

II. SECONDARY SOURCES

Alexandar, Doris M. "Eugene O'Neill and Light On," *Modern Drama*, 3 (1960), 260-67.

——. *The Tempering of Eugene O'Neill*. New York : Harcourt, 1962.

Asselineau, Roger. "*Mourning Becomes Electra* as a Tragedy," *Modern Drama*, 1 (1958), 143-50.

Barlow, Judith E. "*Long Day's Journey into Night* : From Early Notes to Finished Play," *Modern Drama*, 22 (1979), 19-28.

Bell, Daniel. *The Philosophy and Literature of Existentialism*. New York : Barron's Education Series, Inc., 1968.

——. *The Harper Dictionary of Modern Thought*. New York : Harper and Row, 1977.

Bentley, Eric. *The Dramatic Event*. New York : Horizon Press, 1954.

Ben-zvi, Linda. "Freedom and Fixity in the Plays of Eugene O'Neill," *Modern Drama*, 31 (1988), 16-27.

Berlin, Normand. "The Beckettian O'Neill," *Modern Drama*, 31 (1988), 28-34.

Bogard, Travis. *Contour in Time : The Plays of Eugene O'Neill*. New York : OUP, 1972.

Bogard, Travis & Bryer, Jakson R. (Eds.) *Selected Letters of Eugene O'Neill*. New Haven : Yale University Press, 1988.

Brasher, William R. "The Wisdom of Silenus in O'Neill's Iceman," *American Literature*, 36 (1964-65), 180-88.

Broussard, Louis. *American Drama : Contemporary Allegory From Eugene O'Neill to Tennessee Williams*. Norman : University of Oklahoma Press, 1963.

Brown, Crosswell. *The Cure of the Misbegotten : A Tale of the House of O'Neill* New York : McGraw Hill, 1959.

Cargil, Oscar *et al.* (Eds.) *O'Neill and His Plays*. New York : New York University Press, 1961.

Carpenter, I. Frederic. *Eugene O'Neill*. New York : Twayne Publishers, 1964.

Coolidge, Oliva. *Eugene O'Neill*. New York : Scribner's, 1966.

Chaitin, Norman. "O'Neill : The Power of Daring, " *Modern Drama*, 3 (1960), 231-41.

Chatterji, Ruby. (Ed.) *Existentialism in American Literature.* New Delhi : Arnold Heinemann, 1983.

Chaudhri, A.D. *The Face of Illusion in American Drama.* Madras : Macmillan, 1974.

Clark, Barret H. *Eugene O'Neill : The Man and His Plays.* New York : Dover, 1947.

David Riesman. *The Lonely Crowd.* New Haven : Yale Univ. Press, 1961.

Dickinson, Thomas H. *Playwrights of the New American Theatre.* New York : Macmillan, 1925.

Dusenburry, Winifred L. *The Theme of Loneliness in Modern American Drama.* Gainesville : University of Florida Press, 1960.

Engel, Edwin A. *The Haunted Heroes of Eugene O'Neill* Cambridge : Harvard Univ. Press, 1953.

Falk, Dorris V. *Eugene O'Neill and the Tragic Tension : An Interpretative Study of the Plays.* New Jersey : Rutgers University Press, 1958.

Finkelstein, Sidney. *Existentialism and Alienation in American Literature.* New York : International Publisher, 1965.

Frazer, Winifred L. "O'Neill's Iceman ——. Not Iceman," *American Literature*, 44 (1972-73), 677-78.

——. "Revolution in *the Iceman Cometh*," Modern Drama. 22 (1979), 1-8.

Gassner, John. (Ed.) *O'Neill : A Collection of Critical Essays.* New Jersey : Prentice Hall, 1964.

Gassner, John. *Eugene O'Neill.* Minneapolis : University of Minneasota Press, 1965.

Gelb, Arthur Barbara, *O'Neill*, New York : Harper, 1962.

Gould, Jean. *Modern American Playwrights*. Bombay : Popular Prakashan, 1969.

Graff, B. Wilson, *Three Hundred Years of American Drama and Theatre*. New Jersey : Prentice-Hall, 1973.

Granger, Brauce Ingham. "Illusion and Reality in Eugene O'Neill," *Modern Language Notes*, 73 (1958), 179-86.

Griffin, Erenest G. O'Neill and the Tragedy of Culture" *Modern Drama*, 31 (1988). 1-15.

Grimm, Reinhold. "A Note on O'Neill, Nietzsche, and Naturalism : *Long Day's Journey into Night* in European Perspective, "*Modern Drama*, 26 (1983), 331-34.

Hieneman, F.H. *Existentialism and the Modern Predicament*. London : Adam and Charles Black, 1967.

Jaidev, "Realities from the Margins : A Deconstruction of *Mourning Becomes Electra*." *Punjab University Research Bulletin* (Arts), 20 (1989). 25-32.

Jung, C.G. *Modern Man in Search of Soul*. New York : Harcourt, Brace, 1953.

Kaujman, Walter. *Existentialism from Dostoyevsky to Sartre*. New York : Meridian Books, 1957.

Kernan Alvin, B. (Ed.) *The Modern American Theatre*. Englewood Cliffs : Prentice-Hall, Inc., 1967.

Keyan, Rostam. *Being and Alienation*. New York : Philosophical Library, 1981.

Kierkegaard. *Fear and Trembling and the Sickness onto Death*. New York : Doubleday, 1954.

Krutch, Joseph Wood. *The American Drama Since 1918*. New York : Random House, Inc.,1939.

——. *Modernism in Modern Drama*. New York : Ithaca, 1953.

Leech, Clifford. *O'Neill*. London : Oliver and Boyd, 1963.

Mantle, Burns. *American Playwrights to Today*. New York : Dodd, Mead and Co., 1929.

——. *Contemporary American Playwrights*. New York : Dodd, Mead and Co., 1938.

Massa, Ann. "Intention and Effect in *The Hairy Ape*," *Modern Drama,* 31 (1988), 41-51.

May, Rollo, *Man in Search for Himself*. London : George Allen and Unwin, 1953.

Mongia, Sunanda. "Maritial Hell in the Plays of O'Neill," *Punjab University Research Bulletin (Arts)*, 20 (1989), 55-63.

Nethercot, Arthur H. "Madness in the Plays of Eugene O'Neill," *Modern Drama*, 18 (1975), 259-279.

O'Neill, Joseph P. "The Tragic Theory of Eugene O'Neill," *Texax Study in Literature and Language*, 4 (1963), 481-98.

Porter, Laurin R. "*The Iceman Cometh* as Crossroad in O'Neill's Long Journey," *Modern Drama*, 31 (1988), 52-62.

Porter, Thomas E. *Myth and Modern American Drama*. Ludhiana : Kalyani Publishers, 1971.

Presley, Delma Eugene. O'Neill's Iceman : Another Meaning", *American Literature*, 42 (1970-71), 347-88.

Raleigh, John Henry. "Communal, Familial and Personal Memories in O'Neill's *Long Day's Journey into Night*," *Modern Drama*, 31 (1988), 63-72.

——. (Ed.) *The Iceman Cometh*. Englewood Cliffs, N.J. : Prentice-Hall, 1968.

——. *The Plays of Eugene O'Neill*. Carbondale : South Illinois University Press. 1965.

Ready, Robert. "The Play of the Misbegotten," *Modern Drama* 31 (1988), 81-90.

Reinhardt, K.F. *The Existentialist Revolt.* New York : Ungar, 1960.

Robert E. Spiller *et al.* (Eds.) *Literary History of United States*. New Delhi : Amerind Publish Co. Pvt. Ltd., 1963.

Robinson, James A. "Convergence and Divergences : Father and Son in *A Touch of the Poet* and *The Iceman Cometh,*" *American Literature*, 59 (1987), 323-40.

Scheick, William J. "The Ending of O'Neill's *Beyond the Horizon,*" *Modern Drama*, 20 (1977), 293-98.

Sheaffer, Louis. *O'Neill : Son and Playwright.* Boston : Little Brown Company, 1973.

Singh, Tejpal. "*O'Neill*'s Plays : Nightmare of American Dream," *Mainstream*, 28 (1989), 18-20.

Skinner, Richard Dana. *A Poet's Quest*. New York : Russell and Russell, 1964.

Straceman, Henrich. *American Literature in the Twentieth Century*. London : Arrow Books, 1951.

Tillich, Paul. *Four Existentialist Theologians*. New York : Doubleday, 1958.

Tiusanen, Timo. *O'Neill's Scenic Images*. New Jersey : Princeton University Press, 1968.

Winter, S.K. *Eugene O'Neill : A Critical Study*. New York : Random House, 1961.

——. "*Desire Under the Elms* : A Modern Tragedy," *Modern Drama*, 3 (1960), 326-32.